# THE DECLINE OF
# CLASS VOTING
# IN BRITAIN

# THE DECLINE OF CLASS VOTING IN BRITAIN:

## Changes in the Basis of Electoral Choice, 1964–1983

MARK N. FRANKLIN

CLARENDON PRESS · OXFORD
1985

Oxford University Press, Walton Street, Oxford OX2 6DP

Oxford New York Toronto
Delhi Bombay Calcutta Madras Karachi
Kuala Lumpur Singapore Hong Kong Tokyo
Nairobi Dar es Salaam Cape Town
Melbourne Auckland

and associated companies in
Beirut Berlin Ibadan Mexico City Nicosia

Oxford is a trade mark of Oxford University Press

Published in the United States
by Oxford University Press, New York

British Library Cataloguing in Publication Data
Franklin, Mark
The decline of class voting in Britain: changes
in the basis of electoral choice, 1964-1983.
1. Voting—Great Britain—History—20th century
2. Labor and laboring classes—Great Britain—
Political activity—History—20th century
I. Title
324.941'085   JN956
ISBN 0-19-827475-0
ISBN 0-19-827474-2 Pbk

Library of Congress Cataloging in Publication Data
Franklin, Mark N.
The decline of class voting in Britain.
Bibliography: p.
Includes index.
1. Elections—Great Britain. 2. Voting— Great Britain.
3. Great Britain—Politics and government—1964-1979.
4. Great Britain—Politics and government—1979-
I. Title. JN956.F7 1985   324.941'0856   85-4112
ISBN 0-19-827475-0
ISBN 0-19-827474-2 Pbk

Set by Crestun Graphics, Abingdon
Printed in Great Britain by
St Edmundsbury Press, Bury St Edmunds

# PREFACE

In this book we attempt to discover what has happened to British electoral politics in the past twenty years. To do this we employ evidence from surveys conducted after each election held between 1964 and 1983, from which a small number of features of British social life are abstracted and followed over the passage of time. To see how these features have changed, and to estimate the effects of these changes on voting choice, we have to use methods that were originally developed by statisticians for quite different purposes. However, this is not a statistics book, and the exposition of the research methods we employ is designed to be straightforward and accessible to those whose interest lies in politics rather than in numbers. As far as possible the findings are explained in words illustrated by means of diagrams, rather than being given in terms of coefficients.

The book is intended for three distinct but overlapping readerships: (a) students of British government and politics who seek to understand the nature of the changes that have occurred over the past twenty years, the reasons why they occurred, and their likely consequences; (b) students of electoral behaviour in general who wish to understand the dynamics of electoral change, so as to gain insights into the mechanisms of change likely to be present in other countries and at other times; (c) students of research methodology who want to see how traditional survey-analysis methods have been applied to the study of social change, so as to be able to do the same thing in other research areas. But while the book is intended for all three groups, it is addressed particularly to the first of them.

Primarily this is a book about politics in Britain. Its focus is upon the major changes that have occurred in British party and electoral politics since 1964: the decline of Labour party voting, increased volatility of party choices, a rise in minor party voting, and the emergence of new parties.

No book is written in a vacuum, and I owe thanks to those people who stimulated my ideas, provided me with feedback and information, helped in organizing the data, and suggested improvements in the manuscript. The most daunting task throughout the project was data management. With eight surveys to be manipulated and kept track of, my first thanks must go to Ann Mair, of the University of Strathclyde Social Statistics Laboratory, for her patient assistance over more years than I care to remember. Thanks are also due to those who designed and fielded the surveys: Donald Stokes, David Butler, Ivor Crewe, James Alt, Bo Sarlvik, David Robertson, and the Gallup Organization. The studies were kindly made available by the latter organization, the economic and Social Research Council Data Archive at the University of Essex, and the Inter-University Consortium for Political and Social Research at the University of Michigan.

For stimulation, feedback, and a constant stream of information I am as always indebted to Tom Mackie of my own department. Others who helped me refine my ideas include Tony Mughan, Edward Page, Ronald Inglehart, Jerry Moon, Ian McAllister, Richard Rose, Maggie Jordan, Don Studler, David Robertson, Jorgen Rasmussen, Norman Nie, Cees van der Eijk, and Ivor Crewe. The first three of these served as co-authors of papers which form the basis of sections in two of the chapters in this book. Special thanks go to Hugh Berrington, Edward Page, Norton Franklin, and Alex Flisch who read various versions of the manuscript and made numerous suggestions for improvements. Needless to say, remaining errors are all my own.

Essentially the body of knowledge contained in these pages was complete in early 1979. However, I wished to confirm my findings by analysing the post-election survey for that year, which did not become available to me until the autumn of 1982, and integrating it with my previous work took me until the following spring. By the time I had established that 1979 did no more than confirm my earlier findings, another election was already upon us. Clearly this process could have continued indefinitely, so in 1983 I decided not to wait for the full post-election survey to become available. Instead I restricted myself to checking those findings that could be replicated from data collected during the election campaign by the Gallup organization. These data are more limited than the academic surveys upon which this study is primarily based, but they do permit some of the more important analyses to be brought up to date to include this most recent election. These findings are mainly reported in Chapter 6.

The book does not report the detailed findings of each survey: that has already been done elsewhere. Instead it takes those few variables shown in previous research to have been of prime importance, and studies them in depth. In particular, it studies them through two decades of developments that were monitored closely in the surveys. We all know that our world has changed politically since 1964. What this book tries to show is precisely how it changed in the electoral sphere, and why the changes took place.

University of Strathclyde
June 1984

Mark W. Franklin

# DEDICATION

To David Butler and Donald Stokes, who showed the way;
to Richard Rose, without whom this book would not have been started;
and to my wife, Carole, without whom it would not have been finished (yet).

# CONTENTS

# TECHNICAL TERMS

This book employs a number of technical terms. These are carefully explained when the need for them arises. As an aid to later reference, page numbers are given under the entry, 'technical terms', in the Index for the point at which the most important of them are first introduced.

# INTRODUCTION

## Things are not what they used to be

British electoral politics have changed dramatically in the past twenty years of so. In the two decades after 1945 the extent to which parties gained or lost seats from election to election was quite small, and continuity of political patterns was evident even when the government changed hands. During most of this period governments enjoyed relatively stable levels of popularity between elections and, above all, there were only two major parties contending for power. Despite perennial optimism on the part of a small band of Liberal stalwarts, no third party made any significant inroads into the two-party vote until 1974.

Clearly all this has changed since 1964. In the past twenty years, not only have the number of seats gained by political parties varied dramatically from one election to the next, but the degree of electoral support that governments enjoy between elections has begun to vary even more dramatically than their vote counts at election times. Above all, the two-party system can no longer be considered closed to outside penetration. In 1974 minor parties captured 25 per cent of the British votes cast, and by 1983 this had risen to nearly 30 per cent. More importantly, perhaps, in 1974 the Scottish Nationalist Party broke through to major party status in Scotland. Although Nationalism declined once again in 1979, the fact that a new party was able to capture so many votes has had a dramatic effect on our expectations for the future of British politics: it is now taken for granted that the SDP/Liberal alliance could, in favourable circumstances, do at least as well over Britain as a whole as the SNP did in Scotland in 1974.

Of course, electoral politics is not the only area in which British political life has changed dramatically. Twenty years ago undergraduate students of British government and politics were taught that there were three pillars of the constitution: Ministerial Responsibility, Cabinet Solidarity, and the Power of the Government to Command the Assent of Parliament. Indeed, these pillars (or at any rate the last two of them) were still felt to be in place as late as 1979, according to Mezey in his *Comparative Legislatures*. In retrospect it is clear that the first of the three pillars had already crumbled by then, and that erosion of the other two was well advanced (see Norton, 1981). And it is not just our political life that has changed in this period. Almost every aspect of our social and economic systems has seen changes of greater or lesser magnitude. Some of these changes have in turn affected the political system, and we shall have reason to refer to them in coming chapters. The point to be made here is that the great changes that have taken place in electoral politics are only one strand in a complex web of changes that are in the process of affecting our lives in almost every conceivable respect.

So why study change in electoral politics? Is this not quite likely to be a consequence of changes elsewhere in our social, economic, or political systems? The answer is that although the arena of electoral politics is indeed only one of many arenas of change, and one that may well in the end prove to have been affected, if not determined, by changes in some other arena, nevertheless it is very probably the arena of public life about which we know the most. Just as predicting elections is the shop-window of opinion pollsters, at which they prove their ability to 'get the answer right' at vast expense to themselves in order to gain credibility (and so earn lucrative contracts) in areas far removed from electoral politics, so the explanation of electoral behaviour has become something of a shop-window for social science research methods in general. For this reason there has probably been a greater concentration of research effort in this area than any other area of political research. As a result there has been more thought and more analysis. Above all, more data have been collected and made publicly available to interested researchers. So scholars stand a better chance of being able to explain electoral behaviour than many other social puzzles. Moreover, such is the visibility of electoral research that, if we can convincingly explain eletoral change, then perhaps we shall be supported in our attempts to research the reasons for change in other less highly visible (but often more important) areas of public and private life.

Electoral politics is the forum of social research that is at the same time most interesting to and best understood by those who are not social scientists. This is not to say that the average member of the general public would be interested in a book about electoral politics, but merely that interest will be more widespread than in many other areas of social research. So electoral politics provides a vehicle for educating the general reader in the nature of social research, its problems and prospects. It is important that methods such as those used in this book be employed in other areas of public life, to study our systems of education, health care, unemployment provision, and so on. Such research is taking place, but for the most part it is much too poorly funded to yield more than superficial findings. One purpose of this book is to show how intricate social life really is, and how carefully it has to be studied and analysed before anything remotely resembling the truth can be expected to emerge.

## A brief history of electoral studies in Britain

The study of British electoral behaviour over the past quarter century has two complementary strands. The first of these focuses on the public face of election campaigns and results. Often referred to as the 'psephological' approach (although that word in fact has a wider meaning) it concentrates on documenting the context within which an election takes place: the events leading up to it, the manœuvering of major political actors, the organization of the campaign, the issues that made news, and the nature of the debates upon these issues. Finally it focuses on the electoral verdict and its interpretation in terms of the other important themes. Each General Election since 1945 has been analysed in a major study in the psephological tradition, the first by H. B. Nicholas and the rest by David Butler, usually writing with one co-author or another.

The second strand focuses on the private face of election campaigns and results. Entitled the 'behavioural' approach by its proponents, it has its origins in the United States and was not really applied to the study of British elections until the mid-1960s, although some earlier studies in this tradition looked at the nature of election campaigns in two or three individual British towns. This approach concentrates on unravelling the ways in which individual voters reach their electoral decision by enquiring into the effects of upbringing, education, social class, and other characteristics that differ from voter to voter; and contrasting these with the specific influences of a particular campaign in which different issues may again affect individual voters in different ways.

One major characteristic of behavioural studies is their dependence on survey material, and the academic study of British electoral behaviour on a national scale did not really begin until the first academic survey of the British electorate was conducted in 1963.

Although commercial organizations had been polling in Britain since 1937, the surveys concerned only gradually came to include sufficient questions going beyond party preference to enable the reasons for this party preference to be analysed; and not until 1963 was a survey instrument designed which had the specific purpose of studying the reasons why people chose to support the party they did. The first book to employ the findings of such polls was Butler and Stokes' *Political Change in Britain* (1969), a second edition of which appeared in 1974.

It is this second strand within the British tradition of electoral studies that constitutes the background for the present book. The concept of class voting is a behavioural concept, since its measurement depends on our ability to investigate the behaviour and backgrounds of individual voters.

*Political Change in Britain* was indeed concerned primarily with the class background to voting choice, and the way in which this background had come to be established over the previous fifty years or so. Butler and Stokes' book thus constitutes a very appropriate starting point for our own study of the decline of class voting. However, it was not the only one written on the basis of academic studies of electoral choice. In 1983 Bo Sarlvik and Ivor Crewe published *Decade of Dealignment*, which focuses on the Conservative victory at the 1979 General Election. In the intervening years a number of other studies were published that we shall find occasion to refer to in later pages, but these two provide a convenient framework for the present book, because this book concerns itself primarily with the changing nature of voting choice during the period (1963–1983) they straddle.

Butler and Stokes were able to write about the 1964 General Election mainly from the perspective of social class, while Sarlvik and Crewe were able to write about the 1979 General Election mainly from the perspective of issues. Partly this different focus may reflect different research interests which led each team to design survey questions biased towards one or the other point of view. Partly it may reflect the fact that if one concern had essentially been met by the first book, then the second book had to focus on what was left. However, it is legitimate to enquire whether Sarlvik and Crewe could have written a book about the 1964 election that focused upon issues, or whether Butler and Stokes would have been able to detect the same dominant class alignment had their first survey been of the election of 1979. It is one purpose of the present book to show that the two pairs of researchers could not have swapped places in this way because, between

1964 and 1979, the basis of electoral choice in Britain changed dramatically. In 1964 the choice was indeed based largely on class factors, as Butler and Stokes documented so well. By 1979 issues had become at least as important as social characteristics in determining voting choice.

## Class voting and electoral change

If electoral politics in Britain have undergone so radical a change, why attribute this to the decline of class voting? The simple reason is because class voting was given credit for the pattern we had before. As late as 1967 Peter Pulzer wrote that 'Class is the basis of British politics; all else is mere embellishment and detail.' If change is taking place on any significant scale, it can hardly be change in the embellishments and details. Indeed Butler and Stokes were probably the first to point out the emerging trends in electoral politics when, in their first edition (1969), they included a section on the weakening of the class alignment which suggested that this weakening was 'consistent with' all of the strands of change that were outlined earlier in this introduction.[1]

Later writers have gone further and identified these strands with the decline in class voting as though no other explanation were possible (for example, Alderman, 1978, pp. 159-67). We shall show in later chapters that the linkage between class voting and electoral change is a subtle one with several facets – all of which have seen changes, but not all of them in the same direction. Nevertheless, the decline of class voting appears to be the mainspring of change in recent electoral politics, and it is our purpose in the core of this book to sift the evidence for and against this view.

However, there are several problems that need to be resolved before we get to the core. In the first place, no generally agreed measure of class voting exists; yet, in order to measure changes in class voting, we not only need a unit of measurement but one that can be applied repeatedly over the passage of time. So the first three chapters of this book are concerned mainly with the nature of class voting, the ways in which it can be measured, and the changing social context within which

[1] The fact that so subtle and perceptive an analysis could have been published only two years after Pulzer's blanket assertion (and on the basis of data collected, two years before Pulzer went into print) should have served as a complete vindication of the survey method in social research, but some reviewers of *Political Change in Britain* were not impressed.

class voting has taken place. Chapters 4, 5, and 6 constitute the central core of the book. Here we turn to the nature of the voting decision, and the way this has changed over the past twenty years. Finally in Chapter 7 we evaluate a number of competing accounts that might serve to explain the changes we have documented.

## Plan of the book

In Chapter 1 we review Butler and Stokes's approach to understanding the nature of class voting. We describe the social mechanisms thought to sustain it and the differential importance ascribed to these mechanisms. We also introduce the methods of analysis to be employed in the remainder of the book, and some technical terms.

The Butler and Stokes approach constitutes the starting point for our own study of the decline of class voting, but it is not the only possible approach. So in Chapter 2 we investigate three alternative approaches that have received attention in recent years. We show how each of them, though valuable from one perspective or another, would not be suited to the needs of the present study.

Returning in Chapter 3 to the Butler and Stokes approach to voting choice, we then focus on the changing social context within which elections have taken place. Many of these changes have been the result of government policies (for example, towards education and housing). We show how these changes alone would have been sufficient to bring down the level of class voting considerably between 1964 and 1979. The chapter makes it clear, however, that all the changes are inter-related, and have to be measured simultaneously rather than one at a time if their true effects are to be appreciated.

In Chapter 4 we move on to consider problems involved in measuring changes over time, and, in the process of disentangling various contaminating influences, manage to identify the specific period during which the major decline in class voting occurred. On the basis of this finding, Chapter 5 is able to investigate the nature of the decline in more detail, and identify its characteristics and probable implications.

We then raise our eyes to a somewhat broader perspective and, in Chapter 6, go on to inquire what, if anything, has replaced class voting in British elections. The answer appears to be that British voters have concerned themselves increasingly with the substantive issues involved in government and party policies, although alternative explanations are carefully considered. The rise of 'issue' voting turns out to match the decline of class voting, both in timing and in extent.

What happened to bring about this change? In Chapter 7, various proposals made by other writers are considered in the light of evidence amassed in previous chapters, and all are found wanting in one respect or another. Our own proposed explanation is more prosaic than many, but it does have the advantage of being consistent with the picture we have by then established of the nature of the changes that occurred.

Our analysis suggests that changes in British voting behaviour have opened the way to far-reaching changes in the British party system, going beyond anything we have experienced in recent years; although the fact that the way is open for such changes does not guarantee that they will come about.

# 1
# CLASS VOTING IN BRITAIN

## How Butler and Stokes explained class voting

Peter Pulzer's (1967) claim that 'class is the basis of British Politics' is probably the most widely quoted of all assertions about British voting behaviour. Yet it was not until two years after Pulzer wrote that the first edition of Butler and Stokes's (1969) *Political Change in Britain* demonstrated the fundamental social mechanisms involved in the process of class voting. Ironically, as these authors themselves realized (1974, p. 206), by the time of their analysis class forces had already apparently passed their peak in terms of influencing election results. But if we are, in this book, to study the manner in which the decline has come about, we must start from an appreciation of the way in which class forces used to make their dominant influence felt. That is the purpose of the next few sections, which rely heavily upon the Butler and Stokes analysis and findings. However, we do not follow their means of exposition. Because causal models figure so heavily in the remainder of the present volume, we take this opportunity to introduce the conventions involved in these models. So the following sections can be regarded as much as an introduction to causal modelling as an introduction to the findings of Butler and Stokes, who employ a different expository technique.

The theory that underpins their exposition holds that children are socialized into early preferences for particular parties in the same way as they are socialized into moral and other value systems. Butler and Stokes spell out the agents of childhood political socialization in some detail, but they stress that socialization does not stop with the end of childhood. Even during adult life, voters continue to be affected by the multiplicity of face-to-face contacts that take place in work and leisure time. So the agents of political socialization are social groupings of which individuals are members, and which determine whether face-to-face contacts are predominantly with people who vote for one particular political party, or not. Socialization theory is further discussed in the final part of Chapter 2.

## The early home environment

Though children must presumably reach a certain age before they develop political awareness,[1] nevertheless there is an important sense in which partisan preferences are inherited at the time of birth. For it is the type of home that a child is born into, and the party preferences held by existing members of the household, that primarily determine the initial political orientation of the offspring of that household, as expressed on the first occasion that children are old enough to vote. The diagram below illustrates these influences by means of two arrows standing for an effect of each parental characteristic on the initial party preference of their offspring.

| Parents Labour | 0.340 | Child initially |
| Supporters | ------------------▶ | voted Labour |

| Parents Working | 0.297 | Child initially |
| Class | ------------------▶ | voted Labour |

A similar diagram could be constructed to show the effects of middle-class and Conservative-supporting parents. Numerical coefficients above each arrow express the effect in terms of change in the chances of a child's voting in accord with the parental influence,[2] and in this case they show that a child was 34 per cent more likely to vote Labour in 1964 if their parents supported the Labour party than if they did not. Similarly, the child of a working-class home was 30 per cent (rounded up from 0.297) more likely to vote Labour than the child of a middle-class home. The manner in which these coefficients are calculated will be described later in the chapter. Coefficients for the equivalent diagram showing middle-class and Conservative parental effects would be somewhat lower since class effects are strongest for working-class children.

The coefficients in the diagram are, however, only correct when the two influences are taken separately, whereas they are not in fact independent of each other. Many children will have been affected both

[1] Dennis and McCrone found that by the age of 10, 80 per cent of British primary schoolchildren could name the country's main political parties and express a preference between them.
[2] These coefficients (and those in subsequent diagrams) were calculated from the Butler and Stokes 1964 election study by a method (regression analysis) outlined later in this chapter.

by their parents' party and also by their parents' class pushing in the same direction, since working-class parents are more likely than not to have voted Labour (and middle-class parents are more likely than not to have voted Conservative). So we need to revise the diagram to show the manner in which the three influences are linked.

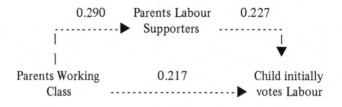

In the second diagram, the influences of Parents' Class and Party are shown to be less than in the first diagram. This is precisely because the two effects are not independent of each other. Since they are in fact connected, when we take either influence by itself it acts as an indicator for the other. Thus, in the earlier diagram, part of the apparent influence of Parents' Party arose from the fact that Labour-voting parents are more likely than not also to be working class; and part of the apparent influence of Parents' Class arose from the fact that working-class parents are more likely than not also to vote Labour. When we take the two influences together we must correct the overestimate that occurs when we take each separately. The corrected influences (0.277 and 0.217) are known as *partial* effects, since each tells only part of the story. In the diagram, we see the partial effect of Parents' Class and the partial effect of Parents' Party. What we do not see is the combined effect of Parents' Class and Party on those children for whom the two partial effects act in concert, but this combined effect turns out to be the sum of the partial effects. Thus a child from a working-class home in which the parents vote Labour was 50 per cent more likely to vote Labour himself (0.22 + 0.28) than one whose parents were neither working class nor Labour voting (rounding up the figures of 0.277 and 0.217 in the diagram).

Thus the linkage between Parents' Class and Parents' Party gives rise to partial effects that are less than the original effects that we depicted in the first diagram (known as *uncontrolled* effects, since each was measured without holding the other characteristic constant); but taken together, their combined influence is greater than either of the original uncontrolled effects.

The linkage between Parents' Class and Parents' Party is important for another reason as well. Without it the influences we have depicted could hardly be referred to as a class-based social mechanism, since the dominant influence was parents' party rather than parents' class. The mechanism becomes class-based precisely because Parents' Party is in part dependent on Parents' Class. Because working-class parents were, in 1964, 29 per cent more likely to vote Labour than were non-working-class parents (0.290 in the diagram), it follows that almost a third of the apparent influence of Parents' Party is in fact attributable to Parents' Class. This is known as an *indirect* or *transmitted* effect, and it undermines the apparent dominance of Parents' Party in two ways. In the first place, the effect asserts that 29 per cent of parents owed their party preference to class background. So party does not add 0.277 but only about 0.2 (some 70 per cent of 0.277) to the determination of Children's Voting Choice. And in the second place, what has to be deducted from the apparent influence of Parents' Party has to be added to the apparent influence of Parents' Class, since its position as prime cause is the reason for the deduction being necessary. So the actual influence of Parents' Class, taking both direct and indirect effects into account, is seen to be 29.7 per cent: exactly what was shown in our first diagram where the two effects were taken separately. But the actual effect of Parents' Party (0.2) is not much more than half what was shown there (0.34) because of its causal position as resulting from Parents Class.[3]

We have spelt out the implications of the causal ordering of these first two characteristics at some length, because the principles involved are fundamental to an understanding of causal models, which are extensively used in this book. There are only three of these principles that need concern us, and they can be summarized as follows:

(*a*) Effects on individuals can be summed. This means that if, as in our second diagram, there are two effects of 0.22 and 0.28 then the combined effect is 0.5 for those individuals who have both of the characteristics concerned (Labour-supporting and working-class parents in our example).

---

[3] Of course, this reassessment of the uncontrolled relationships depends completely on the plausibility of the causal influences depicted in our second diagram. If someone were to assert that parents' party was not consequential upon parents' class, or (even worse) that, because people may misremember their parents' party, parents' class was actually consequential upon parents' party, then the relevant calculation of indirect effects would give rise to a completely different view of the relative importance of the two characteristics.

(*b*)   A characteristic early in causal sequence will have both direct and indirect effects. Because of this, its actual importance will be greater than would have been thought by looking only at its direct influence. For the very first characteristic in causal sequence its total effect will turn out to be the same as its uncontrolled effect.

(*c*)   A characteristic late in causal sequence will appear more important than it really is. Even its partial effects overstate its true importance, since a proportion of these effects would not have occurred but for the effects on it of prior characteristics. Thus Parents' Party appears to be the most important influence on child's voting choice in our second diagram, but, as we have already seen, almost a third of this apparent influence is actually ascribable to the prior characteristic.

### The school environment

A child's first voting preference is affected by more than the home environment. Certainly the type of neighbourhood will be important in determining the sorts of political attitudes that will impinge outside the home, and relatives and friends from outside the immediate neighbourhood may also have an effect, but Butler and Stokes did not investigate these influences. The only other environmental influence on childhood socialization which they measured was that of the school, and this influence was measured in two different ways. In the first place, respondents were asked what *sort* of school they had attended. In 1964 the important distinction was between secondary modern and grammar schools, with a small proportion attending the privately funded and curiously named 'Public Schools' and other independent schools. Since 1964 most schools have become 'comprehensive', but at the time of the first Butler and Stokes surveys there were very few of these. The difference between grammar and secondary modern schools was supposed to be one of academic aptitude, with children who could pass a special exam being accepted into grammar schools and the remainder going to the secondary moderns, unless their parents could afford a private education.

Because of the better employment prospects deriving from a grammar-school education, middle-class parents under the old system were particularly anxious that their children should be successful in being admitted to these schools. For this and many other reasons, children from middle-class homes were over-represented in the grammar-school population and under-represented in the secondary-modern population. So schools of each type had a class ethos that was quite distinctively different from that of the other type. This ethos could reinforce the home political environment (in most cases) or dilute it (in those few cases where children from a home background rooted in one social class attended schools where the predominant ethos derived from the other class). When school and home both pointed a child in the same political direction the result was generally to increase the likelihood of inherited partisanship. Where the two sets of influences pointed in different ways, the likelihood of inheriting parental partisanship was somewhat reduced (Butler and Stokes, 1974, p. 105).

The second way in which school environment was measured was in terms of the age at which each respondent had left school. For those who were educated before the coming of comprehensive schools there was a very strong correlation between type of school and age of leaving, with most secondary modern pupils leaving at the minimum legal age and most grammar-school pupils staying on at school after that age.[4] However, in surveys conducted during the 1970s, the proportion of the electorate for whom the secondary modern/grammar school distinction was relevant has become increasingly smaller with the passage of time. This does not mean that education will have ceased to affect the political orientation of younger age-groups. Even in comprehensive schools there is a degree of segregation between children with good academic prospects and children who are expected to leave at the minimum legal age. And for children who stay on beyond this age, segregation (within the classroom, at any rate) is normal. Such children will mix almost solely with other children who have stayed on after the minimum leaving age.

While measuring the effects of education in terms of this second dichotomy may understate its influence in earlier years, at least we can be relatively sure that it will be measuring the same thing in 1979 as in 1964. Any decline in the effects of education as measured in this fashion will thus be attributable to changes in its impact upon individuals rather than simply a reflection of the smaller and smaller

---

[4] The minimum legal age for leaving school is itself something that has changed over time. Older members of our samples will have had compulsory education only up to the age of 14 (some very elderly members of our samples might have been able to leave school at the age of 12). Those leaving school after these provisions of the 1944 Education Act came into effect and before 1972 will have had to stay at school until the age of 15, while those who left school more recently will have had to stay on until they reached the age of 16.

number of individuals for whom the grammar-school/secondary-modern distinction is relevant. This additional characteristic can be brought into our previous model simply by adding a second loop running from Parents Working Class to Initial Voting Choice, via the new characteristic, as shown below.

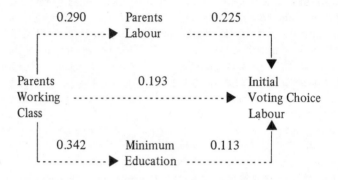

Note that the previous effects of Parents' Party and Parents' Class have again been reduced by bringing an additional characteristic into play, but that total effects on initial voting choice have again been increased, to almost 54 per cent (0.225 + 0.198 + 0.113). But the increase from 50 to 54 per cent in effect on Voting Choice as a consequence of bringing in a third influence is much less than the increase from 34 to 50 per cent that resulted from bringing a second influence to bear. The effects of Education could be said to have been largely anticipated by the effects we considered first. After all, there is a high probability that a child of working-class Labour-voting parents will have had a minimum education. When bringing to bear highly interrelated characteristics of this kind, diminishing returns set in quite quickly.

This brings up the question of how one decides when to desist from elaborating a causal model. Three considerations are relevant to this question. The first is whether the addition of some further effect increases the extent to which we can explain the behaviour under study (in this case, Voting Choice). This is not simply a matter of totting up the total of all effects and seeing how much this has increased, because an effect can be considerable and still not explain very much that we did not already know. This will happen if an effect applies only to a small proportion of individuals. It is not a problem that has arisen in any of the examples we have looked at so far.

The second consideration is one of parsimony: simple explanations and simple models are to be preferred, other things being equal. So a small increase in explanatory power may not be worth the loss of parsimony involved in doubling the number of indirect paths (in our example). On the other hand, a concern for theoretical plausibility may point in the other direction. Though education may add little to other effects, there is every reason to suppose that its relative importance is no less than shown. Its influence is *not* attributable simply to the home environment. In this case, a more parsimonious model would be misleading.

The third consideration is often the most important. In the case of socialization, childhood is not the end of the story. As adults, voters find new influences coming to bear on their political preference which often modify their initial voting choice, and these additional influences may themselves in part be products of earlier features of their lives whose effects, like those of education, might otherwise have been thought to be slight. In particular, people's occupation will be largely affected by their educational attainments, as shown in the next diagram, and occupation has long been considered the defining characteristic of social class in Britain.

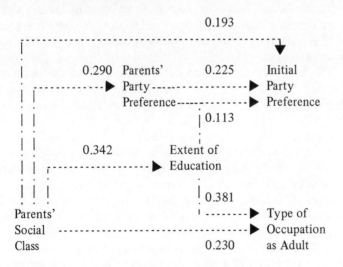

### The working environment

Before moving on to discuss the effects of adult influences on voting choice, it will be hepful if we introduce a few technical terms that will later serve to simplify our discussions. In the diagrams shown above, the arrows representing effects lead from one concept to another. These concepts are sometimes represented as *characteristics* (attributes such as Parents Working Class or Minimum Education, in previous diagrams) and sometimes as *variables* (Parents Social Class or Extent of Education, in the diagram above). A variable is simply a general term standing for any one of a number of alternative characteristics. Thus the childhood class environment of someone responding to a sample survey could be middle class or working class or undefinable, while their parents' party preference could be Labour or Conservative or something else. Childhood Class and Parents Party are known as variables because we expect different respondents to vary in terms of the relevant characteristic. Some will have one characteristic while some will have another. Variables represent concepts that are often quite complex, but the representation of these concepts is usually exceedingly simple, and sometimes simplistic. Even a concept such as parents' party preference has often to be simplified, if we consider that there are generally two parents who might have had different preferences.

In this book the initial letters of variable names are capitalized to distinguish them from the corresponding (unsimplified) concepts. Generally the distinction between a variable and its underlying concept is of no importance, but occasionally it matters greatly which one is being referred to.

The need for simplification derives from the fact that we are not generally interested in the niceties of different effects for small groups of people so much as in the broad picture of influences in general applying to large numbers of people. One day, when our understanding of social processes has advanced considerably, we may be interested in coming back to dot the *i*s and cross the *t*s but in the meantime, as long as we are not simplifying to the extent of actual misrepresentation, these short cuts are necessary in order to permit us to focus our attention on effects and influences that are important because they are widespread, without getting bogged down in embellishment and detail.

With this in mind, it will come as no surprise to discover that social researchers generally treat occupational categories in a rather cavalier manner. There are, after all, literally thousands of distinct occupations, but very seldom are we interested in differences between dentists and doctors, or between electricians and plumbers. Indeed, for many purposes we are content to lump together all occupations considered to be working class on the one hand, in contrast to other occupations considered to be middle class on the other. This is because, as with educational influences, what concerns us is to be able to characterize the political ethos of the workplace in two categories, so as to decide whether a person's occupation will bring them into contact with an ethos that is predominantly Conservative or predominantly Labour.

Occupation is not the only variable that can be employed to represent the dominant ethos of a person's working environment. A subsidiary variable is Union Membership. Although unionization has been spreading into middle class occupations in recent years, nevertheless it is generally a characteristic of working-class life, and membership of a union can reinforce a working-class occupational ethos and so increase the likelihood of Labour-voting.

## The social environment

Butler and Stokes propose two major politicizing components of the social environment in which adults move outside their places of work. One relates to their immediate home environment, and the other to the nature of the area within which they live. A third component of this environment, religious affiliation, was also assessed but found to have little impact on present-day voting choice.

The importance of the home environment in conditioning political behaviour derives from the fact that, in Britain, the type of house that people occupy is, and has for a long time been, conditioned by class and income considerations. Privately-owned houses were traditionally the prerogative of those with more than average wealth and social standing, and new houses have generally been built in 'estates' created by successive waves of expansion as British cities grew. So people buying houses tended to do so in proximity to other people buying houses at about the same time: people with similar income levels and social standing. With the passage of time such housing developments would be overtaken by new construction of more desirable properties further from the city centre, and some of the housing established in the previous wave of expansion would fall into the hands of landlords interested in renting them to tenants without the means (or perhaps without the inclination) for home-ownership. Such areas would then become areas of mixed ownership, with many properties remaining in the hands of owner-occupiers, even while adjacent properties became tenanted by families of lesser means. As housing stock in older parts of cities deteriorated, so the mixture of owner-occupancy and private rental accommodation would change in the direction of more and more rented homes in areas of poorest housing stock. So the natural growth of new housing areas and decay of older housing areas led to segregation by social class of people's places of residence, with middle-class people tending to live in newer suburban areas, and working-class people tending to live in older central city areas; though with extensive areas of mixed accommodation where the decay of housing stock had started but was not well advanced.

Onto this traditional pattern of social segregation was grafted in more recent years the additional segregating influence of council housing. As central city housing stock declined to the point of requiring demolition and replacement, local authorities increasingly shouldered the responsibility for providing accommodation for those who needed rehousing: generally less well-off people who had occupied the private rental sector of the housing market. The resulting publicly financed 'council housing' tended to be built in 'schemes' or 'estates' often suburban in location, but seldom near to the suburban estates of privately-owned houses. Areas with large working-class populations (and generally Labour-controlled local authorities) were particularly likely to become characterized by sprawling council estates in which segregation by class was even more pronounced than elsewhere.

Segregation has political consequences. In so far as class voting exists, it will be reinforced by patterns of residence that limit social contacts between people of different classes. As in the case of educational segregation, we expect social contacts generally to breed consensus, and if such political discussion as may occur around the area of the home (what one might, in a suburban context at any rate, call 'garden fence politics') reinforce the influences of early socialization and the working environment, then there is every reason to expect this to lead to increased conformity of voting choice with class norms.

We have now introduced six characteristics associated by Butler and Stokes with class voting. These can be assembled in a single causal model, as illustrated in Figure 1.1, where the extent of each effect is represented by the thickness of the arrow carrying influence forward to voting choice (instead of the numerical coefficients used in earlier diagrams). Coefficients for the effects represented in this model will be presented in Chapter 5. Meanwhile there are a number of things that have to be said about it on the basis of our discussions in this chapter. First, though, what about the influence of the wider area within which

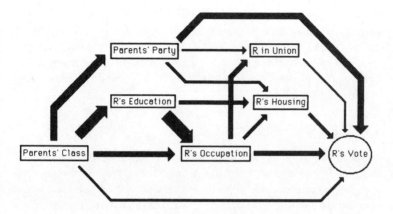

Figure 1.1. Relative importance of paths by which respondent's
social characteristics influenced Voting Choice in 1964
(see Chapter 5)

people live? At the start of this section it was pointed out that the
wider social environment was an important determinant of voting
choice, according to Butler and Stokes, yet it has no place in Figure
1.1. This is because, by the time one takes simultaneous account of all
six of the social characteristics included in this Figure (which Butler
and Stokes never did) there is no room left for additional social
influences. The social character of the area within which people live is
reflected in the housing stock, occupational mix, extent of unionization,
and even types of schools found in the area. Above all, it is subsumed in
the dominant party bias reflected in the powerful effect of Parents'
Party depicted in Figure 1.1.[5] Butler and Stokes compared the voting
preferences of middle- and working-class respondents in mining and
resort areas (1974, pp. 130–7) and found great differences between the
political preferences of people of the same class in constituencies of

---

[5] There is some doubt as to the validity of measuring parental party preference by means of asking respondents about the party preferences of their parents.
It is well documented that respondents have poor recall even of their own past
voting choices where these differ from present preferences. We shall return to this
question in Chapter 3. However, in the present context it is worth pointing out
that the strong links found between constituency partisanship and parental
partisanship suggest that if there is contamination in the measurement of this
variable, it may well be contamination not only from Present Party Preference but
also from Remembered Home Environment. Thus parents may not always be distinguished from other political influences of early childhood. To the extent that
this occurs it is no bad thing, since such influences were otherwise unmeasured.

each type. But in as extensive a model as that depicted in Figure 1.1, such differences do not remain unaccounted for to any significant extent. When measures of constituency-type are introduced into a model already containing the six variables we have been discussing, the additional explanatory power gained thereby is trivial (see also Kelley and McAllister, 1985).

## The model

It should be stressed that while the model depicted in Figure 1.1 is inherent in the exposition of Butler and Stokes, they present no such model. The nearest they come to a causal model of any kind is in a footnote to the first edition (1969, p. 72) of their study, discussing the foundations of self-perceived class. And there can be no doubt that a model such as that depicted in Figure 1.1 does simplify the social reality it seeks to depict far beyond what would be desirable in an introductory exposition. We need the model in order to be able to investigate changes in class voting over time. For a full account of the nature of class voting at the start of our period there can be no substitute for reading the original presentation, but for our present purposes all that is necessary is a brief discussion of some of the most important simplifications incorporated in the model.

Two simplifications were mentioned in the last section: the effects of religion have been omitted because of their small influence on voting choices, and those of the local environment because they turned out to already be subsumed within the variables included. A variable that concerned us earlier in this chapter, Initial Voting Choice, has had to be reconceptualized for a combination of logical and practical reasons. Logically it is hard to place this variable in causal sequence within a model that includes adult characteristics such as occupation and housing that may or may not have been acquired by the time the first opportunity arose for an individual to cast a vote at election time. Logically, also, it is hard to know what to do about individuals whose initial voting preference is the same as their current preference because they are not yet old enough to have voted in more than one election. Really the effect of past voting preferences can only be investigated in a study specifically intended for this purpose, such as the one conducted by Hilde Himmelweit and associates that we shall discuss in the next chapter. However, there is also a practical problem about incorporating earliest voting preferences into a model of the kind depicted in Figure 1.1. This derives from the fact that earlier voting preferences are so closely related to current preferences that there is little left for other variables to explain. Measuring influences of social structure can be subject to bias as a consequence, and when our concern is to represent class influences on voting choice, this is a considerable disadvantage.

Apart from the fact that some variables are necessarily missing, the major simplification inherent in Figure 1.1 is the fact that all the variables represented there are measured in two categories. For example, housing is not divided into owner-occupied, privately rented, and council housing but into only two categories (council or non-council). One reason for this simplification derives from our need to treat all influences equally; and the lowest common denominator of all the characteristics represented in Figure 1.1 is the dichotomy. Other reasons will emerge as we discuss the ways in which we can calculate the actual strengths of effects illustrated in the model. We shall turn to this after we have talked about detecting change.

## Detecting change

This book is about social change, but so far we have said nothing about how change can be measured. Superficial measurement of change is not difficult: one can plot the number of people living in private rented housing at successive elections, for example, and if the proportion changes then change can be seen to have occurred. But even so simple a measure as this can hide as much as it reveals. For example, if a decline is found in privately-rented housing then a question arises as to whether people are moving from one form of housing to another, or whether we are simply observing a more glacial change in living habits, where young householders are no longer entering the private rental market as the older inhabitants of such dwellings die off. In the first type of change, people who once lived in one sort of environment are experiencing new surroundings, while in the second type of change no one moves to new surroundings even though society as a whole is changing. The first type of change is known as a period effect and the second as a cohort effect.

The terms 'period effect' and 'cohort effect' are technical terms in the jargon of social science. The meaning of the first is fairly obvious: the world changes at some period and the people in it (or some of them) are affected by the change. The coming of the Second World War would be a good example of a change that affected the whole British

population. The meaning of the second term is somewhat obscure
unless one understands that a 'cohort' in social research is a segment of
the population that is born within a circumscribed span of time, whose
members pass through life in an unchanging relation to other cohorts
ahead and behind them. Thus the post-war 'baby boom' cohort was
aged between 1 and 5 in 1950. By 1960 this cohort was aged between
11 and 15, and by 1970 it was aged between 21 and 25. At each point
in time its members can be identified by their dates of birth. So a
'cohort effect' is a change that applies to new cohorts as they enter a
population, but does not affect pre-existing cohorts. The rise of the
new 'pop' culture in the mid-1960s is a good example of a change that
mainly affected younger cohorts. The span of time encompassed by a
cohort might be taken as all those born in a single year, all those born
in a particular decade, or all those born between two singular events
such as the two world wars. In electoral studies a cohort is often taken
as the group of voters that first vote at a particular election; but this is
not a universal convention, and the defining characteristics of any
cohort have always to be stated.

A new cohort may, of course, not have all the characteristics that it
will gain later in life. People do change as they grow older, but such
changes constitute 'age effects' and *are not visible* when all cohorts are
taken together, unless the age structure of the society changes dramatically. Thus if most young couples used to start life in rented
accommodation, moving into council houses or their own homes only
later in life, this would constitute an age effect. But unless the proportion of young people were to change, or the age at which they
moved out of privately rented accommodation were to change, this
effect would not show up in a count of the numbers in privately-rented
houses from year to year.

More importantly, age effects cannot be distinguished from cohort
effects within a sample taken at a particular point in time. And period
effects cannot be seen at all within such a sample. Change will only be
evident when that sample is compared with others taken at earlier or
later periods in time. A cohort effect may be noticed, but it cannot be
distinguished from an age effect, because all that will be visible in a
single sample is that older people differ from younger people. This
could be because the younger people came into the population distinctively different from their predecessors, or it could be that as they get
older they will come to resemble what their elders are like now. Once
again, only comparison with other samples taken earlier or later in time

can determine whether change is taking place in the society as a whole or (alternatively) that the nature of a cohort is changing as it ages.

So there are three types of change that have to be distinguished in social research, and they can only be distinguished by looking at samples of the entire population taken at different times. In a sample taken at only one point in time age effects cannot be distinguished from cohort effects. And in successive interviews with the same age cohort (as might occur if the same individuals were re-interviewed in a long-term study of their political development), age effects cannot be distinguished from period effects.

In the remainder of this chapter we become even more technical, and consider the ways in which effects can be measured. This topic is an essential prerequisite for understanding the issues involved in choosing a research approach, and for appreciating the ways in which our approach differs from those adopted by other scholars. So anyone who wants to understand the central part of Chapter 2 will have to read the next section on measurement first. On the other hand, Chapter 2 is not essential reading in order to be able to follow the argument of the rest of the book: any reader who is not interested in why I think alternative approaches inferior for the purposes of this study is invited to skip forward at this point, and pick up the thread of the main story in Chapter 3.

## Measuring effects

When we measure effects we attempt to quantify the extent to which one variable depends on another. The variable whose variation we are trying to explain is thus known as the *dependent* variable. Variables being used to provide the explanation are known as *independent*. Note that a variable in the middle of a causal sequence may be dependent on prior influences but independent of subsequent ones. Although there is no logical reason why two variables should not be dependent on each other (with arrows running both ways between them) such a model is hard to handle computationally; and even then it is critically important to take each effect separately. If we consider two variables $A$ and $B$, the effect of $A$ on $B$ will in general differ from the effect of $B$ on $A$. Which of the two variables we take to be dependent determines which effect we compute, and here what we need is a good theoretical understanding of how the world works. Statistics will not tell us which is our dependent variable.

The effect coefficients whose properties we discussed at length earlier in this chapter are known variously as 'differences in proportions', 'differences of means', or 'best-fitting slopes'. These different terms correspond to different ways of measuring the coefficients, but in most of this book effects are best thought of in a manner corresponding to the first of these terms. For example, the effect of Parents' Class on Respondent's Voting Choice corresponds to the difference between the proportion of Labour-voting respondents whose parents were working class and the proportion of Labour-voting respondents whose parents were middle class. If this difference is found to be large then parents' class will be having a powerful effect, and the chances of a respondent growing up to support the party of his parents' class will be high. If the difference is found to be small then the effect will be weak, and the chances of generational transmission of class political values will be much less. Here the word 'effect' is being employed in a technical way which strictly speaking avoids any causal implications. It would be hard in ordinary English usage to talk of an effect of respondent's partisanship on parents' class since causation could not possibly run that way, but in statistical terminology there are always two effects involved in any relationship (for example, the effect of Partisanship on Class as well as the other way around). Often neither of them involves actual causation.

The three different ways of measuring effects will not come to the same thing unless the variables involved are all dichotomies. Neither will they turn out the same if there are more than two variables in the model. However, all the variables in our model *are* codable as dichotomies, and the differences that result from employing the different methods of calculation in the presence of multiple explanatory variables are very slight in practice (see Franklin and Mugham, 1980, for a demonstration of the tiny differences that arise in a model very similar to the one we presented above; and see Kelly and McAllister, 1985, for another demonstration).

A close relation to the best-fitting slope is the 'regression weight' of a variable, which indicates its relative importance in comparison with other explanatory variables when these are not all measured on the same scale. For most of our purposes the choice between the two measures would make no difference since our variables are generally measured on an identical 0,1 scale: 0 for cases not having some characteristic (Labour-voting parents, for example) and 1 for cases having that characteristic. However, we do have occasion in later chapters to make use of variables measured on other scales, and on such occasions we do employ regression weights to indicate the relative importance of different effects. A regression weight is computed by means of a 'regression analysis', which is also the technique used for estimating a best-fitting slope. The nature of regression analysis is further explored below and in the central section of Chapter 2.

Associated with these means of calculating effects are two further kinds of measure with which we need to have some passing familiarity. The first of these measures the *importance* of an effect in terms of how much it can tell us about variations in the variable we are trying to explain. A powerful effect may not explain much about voting behaviour if it only applies to a very small number of individuals. This situation will be characterized by assymmetry in the two effects involved in the relationship, with the powerful effect in one direction being paired with a very weak effect in the other; and this lack of explanatory power will be indicated by a low 'proportion of variance explained' (the product of the two effects). An alternative and closely related measure is the degree of 'correlation' between two variables. We shall see in the next chapter that while owning two cars does have a powerful effect on the voting behaviour of the individuals concerned, nevertheless, because there are so few two-car owners, the effect tells us little about voting behaviour in general, and the *variance* in voting choice *explained* by two car ownership is small.

The final type of measure, which will concern us very little, indicates the *significance* of an effect. In ordinary English this sounds very like *importance,* but actually in this context it is a technical term that relates to the use of samples to tell us about the world. A relationship found in a sample is deemed to be *significant* if it is unlikely to be the result of happening to pick on one sample rather than another. If an effect is so small (or involves so few individuals) that another sample might fail to show it, then it is not deemed significant, even though the effect might be a powerful one and (in a very small sample) the correlation might also be high. Tests of significance tell us how confident we can be of finding the same relationship in another sample. However, since the samples we use are large enough to yield significant results even with very small relationships, the outcomes of significance tests would be unlikely to interest us in any case. With between 1,700 and 4,200 cases in each of the samples we employ, any relationship important enough to be considered for inclusion in one of our models is bound to be significant.

Even in samples of the size we employ in this study, it would be impossible to calculate differences when as many as six or seven variables were included in a single model. This is because a difference would have to be calculated between two proportions (or means) among groups defined by the correspondence of six other character-istics. Even if each of these characteristics were to split the samples in half, and each resulting group were also to be split in half by all the remaining characteristics, we would end up with groups containing only a handful of members between which differences would be unlikely to be significant even in the presence of powerful effects. So we use the technique of regression analysis to estimate best-fitting slopes by algebraic manipulation of the interrelationships between the variables, according to rules similar to those we employed earlier to work out transmitted effects. Happily, this analysis is done by a computer and the precise fashion in which it is done need not concern us here. What we do need to be aware of is that it is an approximate technique that can give misleading (or biased) estimates where one or other of the proportions being compared is very close to either 0 or 1. But the fact that bias can arise when proportions are close to 0 or 1 has given rise to a fourth method of calculating effects which is called 'log-linear', and to which we shall return in the next chapter. We have already indicated that differences resulting from this bias are small in practice.

The reasons why we employ regression analysis in this study are simple. Each of the alternative techniques has deficiencies that would make it impossible for us to measure one or more of (*a*) effects, (*b*) variance explained by effects, or (*c*) prior influences transmitted by effects in the manner described earlier in this chapter. Yet these are the three things we have to be able to measure if we are to assess the extent of class voting at the start of our period, the nature and extent of the decline that took place in class voting during our period (and if possible the date at which it occurred), and what if anything replaced social class in determining voting choice thereafter.

### Effects of class on voting choice

When the methods described above are used to evaluate the direct effects on voting choice of the variables that were illustrated in Figure 1.1, the results are quite striking. Figure 1.2 illustrates the power of different variables to predict the voting choice of individuals based on a regression analysis of major party voters in the 1964 survey. Each

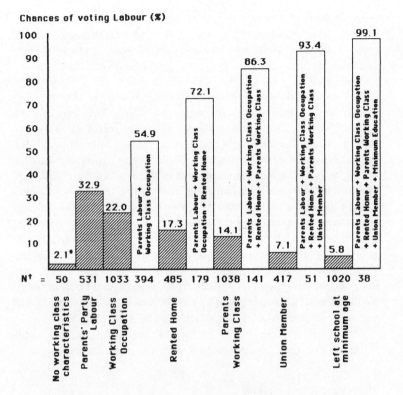

* This constant term is included within each of the other probabilities depicted.

† N's derived from crosstabulation. These are less than the corresponding
regression N's because of missing data treatment in that analysis. Total N
from the crosstabulation was 1208.

Figure 1.2.    Individual and cumulating effects on the probability of
voting Labour due to various working class characteristics, from
regression analysis of major party voters, 1964 (see Chapter 5).

shaded bar in the graph indicates the probability of people voting
Labour if they had one particular characteristic typical of such voters,
but no other. The unshaded bars give the cumulative probabilities of
voting Labour for individuals with successively more Labour characteristics. Thus the right-most bar shows that the probability of voting
Labour for an individual with all the social characteristics associated
with such a vote in 1964 was fully ninety-nine out of a hundred. The
variables could have been taken in any order, but were in fact taken in

order of their importance in structuring voting choice. Thus the left-most variable is Parents' Party, the most powerful predictor of voting choice in Britain, while the first two variables together (Parents' Party and Occupational Class) are shown to be more powerful than all of the remaining four.

Figure 1.2 makes it clear that, at least in 1964, social characteristics were powerful determinants of voting choice. Only 2 per cent of those with no working-class characteristics could be expected to have voted Labour, while less than one per cent of those with no middle-class characteristics could be expected to have voted Conservative in 1964 on the basis of these regression estimates. When all of these reinforced one another in a middle class direction, fully 98 per cent of major-party supporters could be expected to vote Tory in 1964. When all the characteristics reinforced each other in a working-class direction, an even larger proportion of such individuals could be expected to vote Labour. If most British people had found themselves in social circumstances where their voting choice was determined to this extent, then there would have been very little left to explain, and election results would have been foregone conclusions. In fact very few people had *all* the characteristics associated with either social class (only 8 per cent in 1964) and the voting choice of the bulk of the population could hardly be said to have been determined by social characteristics.

### Summary and implications

In this chapter we have described the basic social mechanisms which ensured that British voting was fundamentally class based in the election of 1964. We have also introduced a variety of technical terms and the more common methods of analysis to be used in later chapters.

The most important substantive finding to have emerged from this discussion is that British voting behaviour was, in 1964, characterized at the same time by powerful socializing forces and also by considerable indeterminacy in electoral behaviour. These two characterizations are not mutually incompatible because the indeterminacy resulted from the extent to which powerful socializing forces counteracted each other rather than reinforced each other in the lives of most people. We shall return to the theme of mixed-class characteristics in Chapter 4; but first it is necessary for us to consider alternative ways in which class voting can be conceived.

# 2
# ALTERNATIVE APPROACHES

The approach to understanding British voting choice that we adopted in Chapter 1 is not the only possible approach. Indeed, class has been described as an 'essentially contested concept' by Peter Calvert (1982, p. 209) in that there will always be disagreement as to what precisely it means and how precisely to divide a population unambiguously into classes. This being so, it follows naturally that there will be many different approaches to analysing the nature of class voting.

In this book we are concerned with class as a force that helps to determine voting behaviour, and so we can limit ourselves to considering the methods used by other researchers who tried to use class to explain British elections. And since explanations based on only a single variable have never been able to explain very much about the party allegiances of British voters, we can further restrict ourselves to considering alternative models that bring enough variables to bear to have some chance of explaining a relatively large part of the variation in voting behaviour that we observe in practice.

At the time of writing, there are only three distinct approaches that fit this bill. One is the approach we adopted in Chapter 1, which uses causal modelling to flesh out the insights that were reached by Butler and Stokes using quite different techniques. Apart from my use of this approach only two studies have employed it in Britain, to the best of my knowledge. One of these is the study conducted by Hilde Himmelweit and associates that we shall be considering first in this chapter. A variant of this approach is employed by Paul Whitely, and we consider it at the same time.

The second approach is to ignore the causal structure inherent in explanatory variables, and consider their impact in such a way as to emphasize not those first in causal priority but those with greatest overall impact. This is the approach employed by Richard Rose in several books. It is associated with the use of tree diagrams to display to best advantage the social effects he analyses. This approach is consistent with our own, only yielding a different emphasis on the importance of certain social characteristics in determining voting choice, and we will consider it in the central section of this chapter.

Finally, there is a very different approach employed by Patrick Dunleavy and others, in which the socializing effects of class variables are denied for theoretical reasons, and voting choice is seen to be determined not primarily by the forces of social influence towards conformity among people who mix with each other socially or at work, but rather by rational self-interest applied to a particular view of the state and the economy. Briefly, Dunleavy takes the view that whereas society used to be divided by a *production* cleavage that placed people in one of two groups depending on whether they produced with their labour or with their capital, it has more recently come to be divided by a *consumption* cleavage that places people in one of two groups depending on whether the most important services in their lives (housing, education, health, transport) are provided by the state or by private enterprise. This approach employs some of the same variables as are employed in our own study, but makes different assumptions about how they operate to determine voting choice. And the manner in which effects are estimated is also different. We will consider this approach, which constitutes the major challenge to our own, in the final (and longest) section of this chapter.

### Modelling the nature of voting choice

As implied by the title, the fundamental purpose of *How Voters Decide* is not to detect the most important influences on voting choice so much as to determine the manner in which these influences are transformed into votes. Hilde Himmelweit and her associates are social psychologists who propose a 'consumer' model of voting that tests the idea that individuals choose a party in much the same way as they might choose a car or refrigerator, by weighing up the alternatives and picking the one that comes closest to satisfying their needs, given the outlay of time and attention they are willing to make.

In order to evaluate this hypothesis the authors had to include in their model psychological and attitude variables whose purpose is not to increase the extent of variance in voting choice that can be explained, but to verify that the manner in which other influences have their effect is indeed by way of values and beliefs. From this point of view the model complements the one we employ. It explains (to the extent that it succeeds in its purpose) how other variables come to have the effect they do (see Figure 2.1). It does not identify what these other variables are, or permit them to show their effects to maximum advantage. And it certainly is not suited to examining changes in the effects of social variables.

The study, even in its own terms, has a number of defects, some of which have been pointed out in a review by Patrick Dunleavy. Prime among them are the small size and biased nature of the sample, which was originally selected for other purposes entirely and only started to be used as a source of data on party choice fifteen years after the initial contact with a selected group of London schoolboys. The group was first asked about politics in 1962, and then re-interviewed at the time of each election up to 1974. As Dunleavy points out, the original data set of 600 boys ends up as a longitudinal sample of only 178 men successfully recontacted again and again over the years. And this group is extremely unrepresentative, containing only 31 manual workers and a huge proponderance of middle-class individuals. A secondary problem is that the variables included in the study are not adequate to the task of establishing the primacy of attitudes in determining voting choice. There are simply not enough social background variables for these to have a fair chance of showing their true importance: in particular, neither Housing nor Union Membership are among the variables measured.

Nevertheless, despite its deficiencies, the study does serve two useful purposes from our perspective. In the first place it investigates the manner in which attitudes mediate between social characteristics and voting choice among those individuals for whom attitudes are important. In so doing it provides the necessary background for our own investigation of the relative importance of issues in determining voting choice later in this book. In the second place (and much more importantly) it does detect change. This is referred to at various points during the study, but the most pertinent numerical example appears in Table 5.3 of the study, which reports on an attempt to discriminate between supporters of different parties in 1962, 1970, and 1974 on the basis of their attitudes. The total ability to correctly classify the members of the sample rose from 66 per cent to 78 per cent between 1962 and 1970, and remained unchanged four years later. The finding is particularly significant because it was made when looking at a single age cohort, so it must be either an effect of aging or else a period effect (see discussion on detecting change, in Chapter 1). It cannot be a simple cohort effect or it would not be visible within a single cohort.

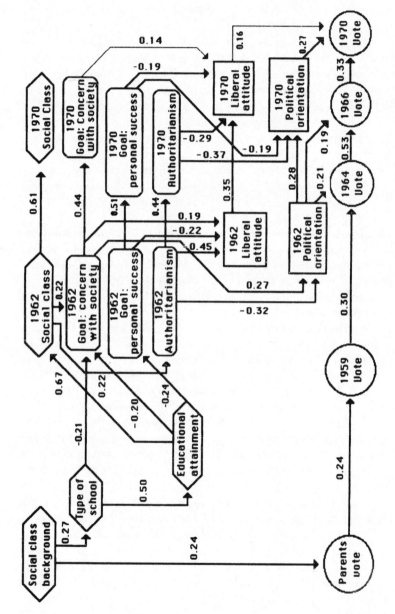

Figure 2.1.    Path analysis of 1970 voting choice. Adapted from Figure 1.3 in Himmelweit et al. (1981)

At the same time, the study clearly is not capable of addressing the issue of major importance to us in this book. It cannot investigate the origins, nature, and extent of the decline of class voting because it looks only at a single cohort and because it does not employ sufficient variables related to class concepts to be able to address the central issues involved. It also employs a model of voting choice designed for the purpose of establishing the nature of linkages between social structure and attitude structure, not for the purpose of establishing the relative importance (and hence change in the relative importance) of these two sets of influences on voting choice.

A variant on the Himmelweit approach is employed in a more recent book by Paul Whiteley (1983) entitled *The Labour Party in Crisis*. Whiteley does not reject the Himmelweit approach and indeed proposes a rather similar model in which voting is made dependent on both respondents' evaluations of the political parties and on respondents' social characteristics. This is potentially much the same model as that employed by Himmelweit and associates, though making use of the far richer attitudinal data available from the 1979 election survey. However, the potential of the model from our point of view is never realized, because Whiteley does not measure the extent to which attitudes are themselves determined by social characteristics. Indirect effects (see Chapter 1 above) are not needed for his purposes. More importantly, the data for so rich a model are not available prior to 1979, thus precluding any comparisons over a period of time.

Both these models have a final disadvantage which should be carefully noted. This is the lack of any attempt to take account of the fact that attitudes may themselves be coloured by pre-existing party preferences. In Whiteley's model, for example, the best predictor of Labour party voting choice is an 'affective evaluation scale' resulting from each respondent being asked to give the party a mark out of ten. This variable correlates 0.63 with voting choice, and by itself accounts for 40 per cent out of the 47 per cent of variance explained by the model as a whole (nearly nine-tenths of this total). Yet this variable will for many individuals not be a cause of Labour voting but a reflection of pre-existing preferences. We shall ourselves have to confront this problem of attitudes being results of party preferences as well as causes when we come to evaluate the effects of issues in Chapter 6.

Since Whiteley is one of the scholars who have sought to explain the changing basis of British voting behaviour, we shall return to consider his analysis further in Chapter 7.

**Depicting social structure**

The second alternative approach that we must consider constitutes a more radical challenge to our own. It employs more of the same variables that we consider important, but it employs them in a subtly different manner with different research questions in view. This is the approach adopted by Richard Rose in *The Problem of Party Government* and elsewhere, in which social structure is viewed as the primary influence on voting choice and is depicted in terms of spreading branches of influence, with the most important influence giving rise to the first split and subsequent influences generating smaller and smaller branches. A typical 'tree diagram' of social influences is depicted in Figure 2.2, reproduced from *The Problem of Party Government*. It relates to the election of 1964, and shows occupational class as the dominant influence giving rise to the first split in the (upside-down) tree, followed by home ownership and union membership in that order.

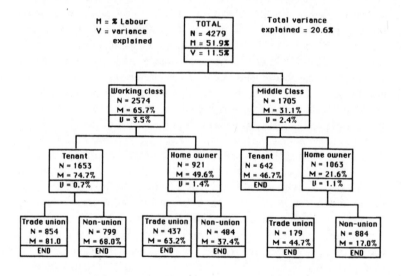

Figure 2.2. Tree analysis of British voting, 1964
Adapted from Rose (1974a)

The approach represented in Figure 2.2 has a number of valuable perspectives to offer. In the first place, since the tree is arranged in order of the importance of different influences, it is easy to see which influence is dominant simply from its position in the tree. In the second place, these influences are measured in terms of variance explained rather than in terms of effects, which makes them even more closely related to actual substantive importance (see discussion of measuring effects in Chapter 1). Finally, although this is not illustrated in Figure 2.1, the approach is well suited to displaying interactions between variables. Had union membership enjoyed less influence among middle-class individuals than among working-class individuals it need not have occurred in second place in both halves of the tree. Some other variable (telephone ownership, perhaps) could have come above union membership among middle-class individuals.

However, the approach is not very well suited to measuring change, and this for quite technical reasons that we shall now describe briefly.[1] Readers who are willing to accept my word for it, and who do not feel at home with technical discussions, are invited to pass on to the next section of this chapter.

We shall take as our example the changing power of occupation to structure partisanship in the late 1960s. Surveys conducted after 1966 provided support for an argument that occupation had become a weakened force in British electoral politics. This was pointed out not only by Rose but also by Butler and Stokes (1974, pp. 203–5, 47–8) and Crewe, Sarlvik, and Alt (1977, pp. 168–81). These studies differ only in their interpretations of the decline. In particular, although this is incidental to his thesis, one of Rose's tables shows not just a decline, but the actual disappearance of Occupation as a predictor of partisanship in 1970, while the other two studies show it to have continued to exert an important, although diminished, effect in this year.[2]

---

[1] The discussion that follows is based on research carried out with Anthony Mughan, now of University College, Cardiff, and published in the *American Political Science Review* (Franklin and Mughan, 1978). I am grateful to my co-author and to the *Review* for permitting me to make use of extracts from that article. The data analysed here are not derived from the post-election surveys which form the basis for the rest of this book but from a series of pre-election surveys conducted by the Gallup Organization in 1970 and employed by Rose as the basis for his study.

[2] It is important to recognize here that Rose himself at no point concludes that social class ceased to have an important effect on electoral behaviour in 1970. In his view, occupation is only one of several dimensions of social class (Rose, 1968, pp. 143–52). He accords it analytic primacy in examining its effects together with each of a number of other socioeconomic measures (Rose, 1974a, pp. 33–47). Having elaborated on the conjoint effects of occupation and other indicators of class (as he views them), Rose then introduces a multivariate analysis to summarize the effects of all the variables examined. It is in this final reduction that Occupational Class is seen to disappear as a predictor of partisanship in 1970

Tree analysis is conducted in stages, and in what the statisticians call a 'stagewise' analysis much depends on the order in which variables are considered. In tree analysis the order is determined by a set of considerations to be outlined below. In 1970 these considerations led Occupation to be considered only after the influence of other variables had been taken into account, and in this situation it added nothing to the amount of variance explained. The result is a parsimonious prediction of voting choice in that it involves the smallest number of independent variables, but when our concern is to trace changes in the explanatory power of a particular variable, such an approach may not be appropriate. The particular multivariate technique that concerns us here is performed by a computer program known as the Automatic Interaction Detector. This technique achieved an important place in research conducted in political sociology during the late 1960s and early 1970s. The strengths of the technique are indisputable (see Sonquist *et al.*, 1971). However, its weaknesses have not always been adequately recognized. Therefore, a brief discussion of how the program works will be helpful to our later discussion of its weaknesses.

As its name implies, the AID computer program was originally developed to detect statistical interaction (explained below) between intercorrelated predictors of some phenomenon (the dependent variable). The program's analytical procedure starts by taking the first specified predictor (independent variable) and looking in turn at every combination of categories of that predictor that splits the data set into two mutually exclusive groups. Each of the resulting dichotomies will give rise to a difference of means for the dependent variable (see Chapter 1) that explains some proportion of the total variance in this variable; and the split corresponding to that dichotomy explaining more variance than any other is remembered by the program which then repeats the search procedure for all of the remaining predictor variables.

After examining each predictor in this way, the program can decide which binary split on which independent variable explains more variance than any other possible split. This optimum split then serves as a criterion for the notional division of the total data set into two subsets. If we imagine the full data set to constitute the trunk of a spreading tree, this first split can be visualized as giving rise to two

(p. 48). In the context of this general approach, such findings imply no more than that 1970 saw a change in the relative importance of various socioeconomic determinants of partisanship. Our own interest in the present context lies in the behaviour of Occupation as a variable in the multivariate summaries.

branches. In the next stage, the program examines each notional branch in turn, determining by the same search procedure which binary split on which predictor explains the largest amount of the residual variance in each subset of the data. Because the subsets are examined independently, the predictor variables splitting each of them need not be the same. When subsets at the same level of the tree are split by different predictors, interaction can be seen to be taking place with the importance of a variable differing according to the presence or absence of other factors. The program continues to split branches until none of the predictor variables is able to decrease the amount of unexplained variance in any of the several subsets of the data by an amount statistically significant at a prespecified level.

Applying AID to party choice in the 1959, 1964, 1966, and 1970 General Elections, Rose found that 1966 produced a clear change in the pattern of the relationship between social structure and voting choice. In the two previous elections, the AID trees showed little in the way of interaction. In addition, they indicated that Occupation was by far the best predictor of party choice in these elections. But in 1966 there was a clear break with this pattern. Not only was the tree asymmetrical in this third election, but also the full sample split first on type of home tenure rather than on Occupation, and the two tennancy subsets then split differently: those in rented homes being distinguished best by Occupation, while home-owners were best differentiated by Union Membership. Dissimilar splits also characterized later branches of the tree. More important for our purposes, however, is the fact that Occupation had not only lost its 1959 and 1964 position as the most powerful predictor, but it had also dropped out of one side of the tree altogether. It now appeared to contribute only 1.7 per cent to the variance explained in Party Choice instead of the 12.4 and 11.9 per cent that it had explained in the 1959 and 1964 surveys respectively. A similar analysis of 1970 voting choice showed Occupation not to appear in the tree at all.

However, to place these findings in perspective, it is necessary to remember that AID's analytical procedure operates stage by stage to remove from the sample all variance explained by the predictor variables upon which the data set is split. Consequently, other predictors that happen to be correlated with the 'best' predictor at each stage in the analytical procedure have no opportunity to claim some portion of this variance. Thus in the case of two powerful but interrelated predictors, one of them will have its explanatory power underestimated so that it will appear lower in the tree or even fail to appear at all. It will fail to appear when the variance left for it to explain after the first split is seized by other predictors with which it is also correlated but which at each stage explain more variance in the dependent variable.

We shall now show how Occupation came to be underestimated in 1966 and how it failed to appear in the tree in 1970.

When all predictor variables were split into two groups, type of Home Tenure proved to be the most powerful one in 1966, explaining 9.2 per cent of the variance in partisanship as indicated in Rose's tree diagram (Rose, 1974c, p. 496). What the tree does not show, however, is that in bivariate terms Occupation explained as much as 9.1 per cent of the variance in partisanship. To say the least, this difference is marginal and, even with a sample of more than 6,000 respondents, it is well within the range of sampling error. Thus a different sample might well have reversed the bivariate impact of these variables with the result that the AID analysis in this year would have split first of all on Occupation, as in 1959 and 1964. Had this been the case, the explanatory power shared by the two variables would all have been attributed to Occupation. This variable would then have appeared to explain more than 9 per cent of the variance in Voting Choice, leaving Home Tenure with rather less explanatory power than it had enjoyed in 1964.

So the 'stagewise' nature of the analytical technique embodied in the AID procedure can have quite serious consequences when attention is focused on changes in the explanatory power of any particular variable included in a series of analyses. The decline in the predictive power of Occupation is beyond dispute, but by 1970 it had not disappeared. This is shown in the bivariate correlations between Occupation and Party Choice in the elections held between 1959 and 1970. Table 2.1 presents these coefficients, as well as the proportion of variance in

Table 2.1.  *Correlations and Variance Explained in Labour Vote by Occupational Class, 1959–70\**

|                             | 1959 | 1964 | 1966 | 1970 |
|-----------------------------|------|------|------|------|
| Correlation with Labour vote | 0.35 | 0.34 | 0.30 | 0.23 |
| Variance explained %        | 12.5 | 11.5 | 9.1  | 5.5  |
| Decline from year to year % |  0.9 |  1.3 |  3.6 |      |

\* The 1959 and 1964 correlations have been calculated from the original trees found in Rose (1974a, pp. 494–5).

partisanship explained in each election (the square of the bivariate correlation) and the decline in this percentage from year to year.[3]

This table shows first that the correlation between occupation and partisanship persisted in 1970. Secondly, in contrast to the implications of the AID analysis that a relatively larger decline in its importance took place between 1964 and 1966, the table shows that the decline was most pronounced between the elections of 1966 and 1970.

But bivariate coefficients are inadequate substitutes for multivariate analysis because they ignore the fact that occupation is not the only important predictor of partisanship. Nor is it completely independent of other social structural predictors, as we have already indicated. A more balanced perspective of the importance of occupation from one election to the next, therefore, would be gained by ascribing to each predictor an importance commensurate with its unique explanatory power, together with a due proportion of the power that it shares with other variables. Several techniques offer the potential of such a perspective, but we have chosen to employ multiple regression analysis.

Like AID, multiple regression is a particular application of the General Linear Model. When used in a search procedure to find an optimum set of predictor variables, AID is in effect being employed as an analogue to what is referred to as a 'stepwise' regression analyses. But the techniques differ in important respects. When multiple regression is used in this manner, it can find, in turn, each independent variable that explains most residual variance in the dependent variable. But, unlike AID, the data set is not split on the variables once they have been identified. Instead, an estimate of their impact is calculated over the whole data set. For this reason, the explanatory power that each shares with others can be apportioned between them according to the weight of each in the analysis (Draper and Smith, 1966, p. 175).

When multiple regression is used to estimate simultaneously the explanatory power of the independent variables found by Rose to be consistently important predictors of party choice, the results are not the same as those generated by the AID program. The two sets of results are presented in Table 2.2. Only those variables are included which appeared in at least two of Rose's 1959, 1964, 1966, or 1970

[3] To maintain comparability of our results, the independent variables in all correlation and regression analyses in this section are the same binary variables as those generated automatically by the AID program. For all variables, the category containing more Labour voters has been coded 1, and the other 0. As was customary at the time this research was conducted, respondents not voting either Labour or Conservative were excluded from the analyses.

Table 2.2.  Comparing Predictors of Partisanship: AID and Multiple Regression Estimates, 1966 and 1970 (Percentages)

| Independent variable (Labour-characteristic) | 1966 | | | 1970 | | |
|---|---|---|---|---|---|---|
| | AID I* Tenancy automatically entered first | AID III Class constrained† to enter first | Regression | AID I Tenancy automatically entered first | AID III Class constrained† to enter first | Regression |
| | (Variance explained) | | | (Variance explained) | | |
| Tenancy (tenant) | 9.2 | 5.3 | 6.5 | 7.1 | 4.8 | 5.3 |
| Class (working) | 1.7 | 9.1 | 4.1 | – | 5.3 | 1.8 |
| Union (member) | 3.4 | 2.1 | 4.4 | 3.3 | 1.0 | 3.4 |
| Telephone (none) | 1.4 | – | 3.3 | 1.6 | – | 2.6 |
| Total variance explained | 15.7 | 16.5 | 18.3 | 12.0 | 11.1 | 13.1 |

* Two variables that appeared in Rose's 1966 AID tree are not included in this table.
† In order to derive coefficients with class entered first, the program was constrained to split first on occupational class even though in two categories this variable explained less variance than tenancy. This constraint is an available option in the AID III program; it was not available to Rose when his earlier analysis was conducted.

trees. In order to achieve comparability between these results, we have used the regression weight of each predictor to calculate a co-efficient which, in the context of this particular analysis, can be safely interpreted as the proportion of the explained variance attributable to that variable when it is given its due proportion of the explanatory power it shares with other variables, in addition to that part unique to itself.

Table 2.2 emphasizes that the methods of assigning shared variance embodied in the two analytical techniques provide different estimates of the relative explanatory power of predictor variables both in 1966 and in 1970. Particularly noticeable on the left-hand side of each half of the table is AID's extreme sensitivity to the order in which inter-correlated predictors are entered into the program. Regression's procedure of averaging shared explanatory power can be seen as being in some sense more reliable.

In addition to highlighting the deficiencies of AID when attention is focused on a single predictor, the table also points to the deficiencies of bivariate analysis. We stated earlier that Occupation and Home Tenure explain about the same amount of variance in (and hence have very similar correlations with) Labour voting in 1966, but Table 2.2 shows that, in regression terms, Home Tenure had more predictive power than Occupation in that election. The different interpretations afforded by the bivariate and multivariate analyses can be explained by the fact that Occupation is more highly intercorrelated with other independent variables than Housing is, so that when this shared variance is averaged over all four predictors its explanatory power is reduced by a greater amount than that of tenancy (cf. Gordon, 1968).

But perhaps the most important single feature of this table from our point of view is that the 1970 regression analysis shows Occupation to have continued to have a place in predicting partisanship in that year, even in multivariate terms, although its predictive power did decline. Its disappearance from Rose's tree for 1970 (1974a, p. 497) was an artifact of AID's method of assigning shared variance.

This exercise suggests a solution to the AID problem, which is to display a series of trees in each of which a different variable is made to appear first, as has been done by Sarlvik and Crewe (1983). Such a procedure does overcome the major disadvantages we have outlined in previous pages, though at the expense of considerable verbosity. The solution does not respond to a shortcoming we have yet to mention.

AID has one final disadvantage more important than any other from the perspective of this book. It does not provide coefficients that can be employed in causal models of the kind that were introduced in Chapter 1. Yet without such coefficients we can never investigate causal processes or the changes in causal processes. The AID perspective places most emphasis on variables that come out at the top of a tree because they explain more variance than any other variable in the phenomenon under investigation. The perspective ignores the fact that some explanatory variables owe part of their force to other variables prior in causal sequence, and that those prior variables must be credited with additional influence over what is directly measurable because of the influences that flow indirectly via other variables. AID could be used to provide such a perspective by splitting first on variables first in causal sequence instead of splitting first on variables with most direct influence, but this use of the technique falls outside the tradition in which it has generally been employed. Used in such an alternative fashion, AID's imperialistic procedure of ascribing to the variable first in the tree all the variance that might otherwise have been shared with other variables comes to the same thing as ascribing back to the variable first in causal sequence the effects it has through other variables. But to use it in this way it must be controlled (as regression analysis must be controlled) by a strong theory about causal priorities in the social process under investigation. One cannot hand over control to any automatic procedure to decide what variable is first in causal sequence.

Figure 2.3 illustrates the use of a controlled tree diagram to display the causal model that was presented in Figure 1.1. Used in this fashion the tree diagram does provide a useful complement to our own approach, since the cumulative consequences of combinations of characteristics can more readily be appreciated. However, its utility is purely as a heuristic device. The coefficients it displays are subject to considerable bias towards the right-hand side where each is based on very few individuals falling into particular combinations of categories. And they cannot be employed, as we shall later use the coefficients of our causal model, in any attempt to further unravel the causal processes involved. So even this use of the tree diagram has no further part to play in our study.

In general we can say that in AID, as in regression analysis, there can be no substitute for a well-founded theoretical understanding of social processes. But theories can be wrong, and if we are wrong about the mechanisms that were illustrated in the model introduced in Chapter 1 then neither regression analysis nor AID will save us from calculating

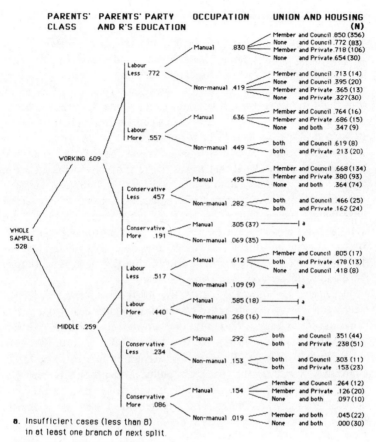

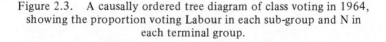

a. Insufficient cases (less than 8) in at least one branch of next split.

b. Next split yields trivial differences.

Figure 2.3. A causally ordered tree diagram of class voting in 1964, showing the proportion voting Labour in each sub-group and N in each terminal group.

*Source*: 1964 election study.

misleading coefficients for the effects of the variables depicted therein. Neither Rose nor Himmelweit dispute the basic theory that underlies that model, but there are political scientists who do dispute it, and their approach constitutes the most radical alternative to our own. We turn to it in the final section of this chapter.

## The consumption cleavage approach

In the past few years, the development and application of the concept of the 'consumption cleavage' has become a modest growth industry in the social sciences.[4] Contemporary consumption cleavage theory emerged within Marixist urban theory which expressed dissatisfaction with the notion that the distinction between capital and labour was the sole determining cleavage for social and political conflict (see Castells, 1978; and also Saunders, 1981 for a discussion of the origins of the consumption cleavage approach in urban studies). While traditional Marxist theory postulated that it was the relationship to the means of *production* that was crucial in determining social and political conflicts, authors such as Castells argued that *collective consumption* processes surrounding the provision of housing, health, and education, for example, also create cleavages. The theory goes on to suggest that the location of an individual within this process helps to determine the manner in which he or she will be affected by state policies concerning these goods and services, as we shall see below.

In general, the approach is attractive for two main reasons. First it claims to explain a wide range of political phenomena, from voting behaviour (Dunleavy 1979) and the process of individual attitude formation (Saunders 1982) to the formulation of national party programmes (Dunleavy 1980a, p. 78). Second, it appears to be highly innovative. It implies that for years political scientists have been employing concepts and terminology derived from a conception of political and social conditions as they existed many years ago to explain phenomena such as voting behaviour, and have largely overlooked the fundamental transformations in social structure of the past twenty years (Dunleavy, 1980a, p. 57).

The approach as applied to the wider field of urban studies shows great promise of asking new and interesting questions. However, when applied at its current level of theoretical refinement to the study of voting behaviour it seeks to give a new set of answers to old questions, and in doing so casts doubt upon the validity of orthodox approaches to the explanation of individual voting intentions. This doubt undermines a number of the most important 'middle range' theoretical

---

[4] This section is again based on research conducted with a co-author: this time Edward Page, now of the University of Hull (Franklin and Page, 1984). I am grateful to my co-author and to Butterworths the publishers for allowing me to use the results of our joint researches in this chapter.

propositions established in the past thirty years of careful empirical research. Our understanding of such important concepts as issue saliency and integration, and such important relationships as that between social stratification and political cleavages (in so far as these affect voting behaviour) are both put into question by the consumption cleavage approach. Above all, our understanding of the nature and function of socialization processes, by which we mean the influence of social milieu in communicating values, attitudes, and patterns of behaviour from person to person not only during childhood but throughout adult life as well (see Kavanagh, 1983, p. 47), cannot survive intact in the face of the alternative view of political processes inherent in the consumption cleavage approach.

Since the foundations of the model presented in Chapter 1 rest upon a conventional view of socialization processes, the consumption cleavage approach represents the most radical alternative of the three we consider in this chapter. But the discussion that follows is important not only in defending the basic assumptions upon which this book rests. If consumption cleavage theory is right, then much of what we thought we understood about human behaviour is wrong; and the implications of this confrontation extend far beyond voting studies or even political science, to fields as diverse as anthropology and social psychology as well.

In the remainder of this chapter we describe our understanding of the term consumption cleavage and introduce some general problems in the conceptualization of this term. We then focus specifically on the question of electoral behaviour and suggest that the consumption approach does not adequately set out how 'objective' differences in life chances associated with these cleavages are translated into party preferences. Next we describe the manner in which orthodox scholarship would approach these questions, and ask whether the consumption approach explains additional aspects of voting behaviour that existing theories do not. Finally we provide a critical test of the value of consumption cleavages in electoral studies.

By offering criticisms of the consumption cleavage approach to voting behaviour we are not seeking to undermine the whole endeavour of exploring the social and political consequences of different modes of consumption and dependence upon state services. Neither are we suggesting that the electoral implications of consumption differences are to be doubted on a priori grounds. Rather we are suggesting that the way in which consumption cleavage theory is now being applied in the field of electoral studies forces on us with little justification a particular view of the relationship between objective interests and voter preferences which is incompatible with orthodox theories of party choice.

## Consumption processes and political cleavages

According to consumption theorists, the key distinction within any particular consumption process is whether one is dependent upon the state for the provision of this good or service, through public housing, education, transport, and the National Health Service, or whether one makes provision for consumption within the private sector through owning a house and car, or by paying for a private health insurance scheme or for private education. As Dunleavy states:

The most important implication of the growth of the public services for the social structure has been the emergence of sectoral cleavages in consumption processes, by which we may understand social cleavages created by the existence of public and private . . . modes of consumption (1980a, pp. 70–1).

A policy, for example, of maintaining the tax relief that an individual may have gained for his mortgage is in the interests of owner-occupiers, and attempts to remove it are against these interests. In short, policy decisions in each of the major consumption areas frequently pose questions involving conflicting interests, benefiting those in one consumption location, as it were, against those in another.

But the fact that there are so many sources of consumption cleavage gives rise to a fundamental problem. As soon as one looks beyond home-ownership to the other consumption processes that bifurcate into state and private provision, it is hard to see how consumption theorists can reconcile the different political responses to broader issues that might be found, for example, in the large number of people who own a car and rent from a local authority. Of the 1,893 individuals in the 1979 Essex election sample, 13 per cent fell into this category, while a further 17 per cent were home-owners without private transport.

When more than one consumption location has been employed in the same analysis, some researchers (for example, Edgell and Duke, 1983) have simply created an additive index of the number of private (or state) consumption processes each person engages in. Others (for example, Dunleavy) have created an implicit typology of contingent locations. Either procedure amounts to measuring the extent to which individuals approximate to the 'ideal type' at one or other extreme of these processes. This might seem reasonable, especially since it is the same procedure as has been adopted by analysts of conventional class effects (for example, Rose, 1974b, p. 510) for many years; but it is not reasonable where the perception of consumption locations and their implications is supposed to be automatic. Class effects can be added, because they operate in the context of a socialization theory that relates attitudes to the number of face-to-face contacts of different types that regularly occur for different individuals. Someone with several working-class characteristics mixes with more working-class individuals than another person with fewer such characteristics. Indeed, the fact that these effects *are* additive serves to suggest that socialization mechanisms do apply in the realm of voting studies. But the socialization mechanism is explicitly eschewed by the consumption theorists, as we shall see below, so it is not clear why different consumption locations should operate on individual attitudes in an additive fashion. If each of the conflicting locations is supposed to have policy implications obvious enough to require no intervention by other individuals to make them clear, then it would seem at least as reasonable to suppose that conflicting consumption locations would lead to cross pressures and even to psychological distress which should in turn (if the psychologists are to be believed) lead many of these individuals to withdraw from the source of distress: the political arena. So it would be primarily 'ideal type' state or private consumers who would remain to participate in politics, which is contrary to casual observation and to the data presented by the consumption theorists (see for example Edgell and Duke, 1983).

## Political cleavages and electoral behaviour

Even if we leave aside the problem of cross-cutting cleavages, a profound theoretical problem arises when we come to consider how consumption cleavages may manifest themselves in political cleavages. Consumption theorists hold that the cleavage differentiates between people dependent upon the state for certain services and people who make private provision for the same or similar services. These can be treated as coherent groups since individuals in the same consumption location will be affected in similar ways by state policies and, at least objectively, they will share the same interests with regard to these policies.

Undoubtedly the life chances of individuals are affected by their consumption locations. However, how do these objective inequalities in life chances affect voting behaviour? Dunleavy's analysis suggests that they serve to fragment the class divisions based upon production, and produce voter alignments based upon consumption cleavages. So much does he hold this to be the case that 'the independent effect of consumption locations on voting appears to be comparable to, indeed slightly greater than, the effects of social grade' (Dunleavy, 1980, p. 79). While Dunleavy does not fully reject the validity of explaining voting behaviour in terms of production-based voter alignments, he argues that 'voters can be seen as aligned instrumentally towards the party most clearly identified with the interests of their consumption location' (1980, p. 78).

This is where the conflict between the consumption cleavage approach and existing theories of electoral behaviour becomes apparent. Existing research provides no evidence to support the presence of a mechanism which would ensure that people became aware of their 'objective' interests. Indeed, even Marxists recognize this problem in the form of 'false consciousness' and admit the need to mobilize the masses into an understanding of the nature of their true interests. Thus while there can be little doubt that consumption locations create different social groupings in this country, and so can be seen as a factor contributing towards social stratification, there is no necessary link between stratification of this kind and political cleavages.

The term 'cleavage' implies, at least in the context of political science, a social or cultural attribute which defines the protagonists in a political conflict. Thus one might speak of a class cleavage or a religious cleavage shaping the ideologies of parties in a political system, as well as defining their potential supporters (Duverger, 1954). That not all *potential* bases for political cleavage are actually found within empirically observable political conflicts underlies Schattschneider's discussion (1960) of the 'mobilization of bias', as a means of determining which conflicts are actually given political expression. Indeed, one of the distinctive contributions that political science has made to the social sciences has been in its treatment of the relationship between social stratification and political cleavages, especially electoral alignments, as problematic. Scholars such as Sartori (1969), Rokkan (1970), and Kirchheimer (1966) stress a variety of factors which mediate the expression of social cleavages in political conflicts, ranging from the conditions prevailing at certain periods in a nation's history when the social cleavage emerged, to the behaviour of political élites who seek to build support by either exploiting or playing down the objective cleavages within an existing social structure. We must, therefore, be cautious when identifying a 'new' basis for social stratification about ascribing to it the ability to determine the nature of political conflicts.

## Socialization and issue saliency

There are in fact two ways in which orthodox political science would seek to link a potential basis for political cleavage with an actually observable political conflict. The first of these is through the cleavage manifesting itself in terms of an issue of high salience, which divides the parties in such a way as to make it possible for party choice to be based upon it (Campbell *et al.*, 1960; Butler and Stokes, 1974). The second is through a socialization process whereby the individuals comprising each group separated by the cleavage in question are led to identify with each other in opposition to those in the other group, so that the cleavage becomes a means of reinforcing other differences (especially political differences) between the two groups (cf. Lijphart 1975).

In the case of issue saliency, the mechanism requires that the issue be more salient than alternative issues competing for the attention of the electorate, and also that political parties be perceived as taking different stances on the issue in question. These two preconditions may indeed have existed at times for issues related to consumption cleavages, but they are not consistently present. In fact, even in 1979 (when housing was certainly an issue that divided the parties) only 8.6 per cent of respondents ranked it as 'the most important question' in helping them to decide how to vote. This compares with 9.1 per cent placing the European community in first place, 12.3 per cent placing nationalization in first place, and 15.1 per cent placing wages in first place as issues that would help to determine their vote.

In the case of socialization, the mechanism involved concerns the tendency of individuals to mimic the behaviour of those who surround them. So a child growing up in working-class surroundings is likely to absorb the values and mimic the preferences prevalent in those surroundings. And in adulthood these values and preferences will either be reinforced by surroundings consonant with those of childhood, or diluted by influences that contrast with those of early socialization. This mechanism is explicitly rejected by Dunleavy who finds it unreasonable to suppose 'that political alignment brushes off by rubbing shoulders in the street' (Dunleavy, 1979, p. 413).

Dunleavy's characterization of the socialization process is not, of course, the same as the way in which researchers in the orthodox tradition describe the mechanism they think is at work. Writers such as Rose (1980), or Butler and Stokes (1974), would stress the role of face-to-face contacts in socialization processes, with individuals copying the attitudes of those with whom they live and work in much the same way as they might copy patterns of dress and speech, as a consequence of the deep-seated human desire for conformity. This is the same mechanism first detailed in William Graham Sumner's *Folkways* (1916) which underpins most of learning theory in Social Psychology, the study of mores in Anthropology, and small group theory in Sociology, before we even start to list the ways in which contemporary Political Science is beholden to it for our understanding of participation, legislative norms, the bureaucratic phenomenon, and presidential decision-making, to mention only a few high points. Nevertheless, this has to be the target that Dunleavy has in mind. The more general phenomenon of 'contagion' to which the quoted passage explicitly refers is no more than the combined impact of many socializing forces at work to reinforce each other in socially homogeneous communities (Butler and Stokes, 1974, p. 133). Indeed, Dunleavy states elsewhere (1980c) that the purpose of his structural model was 'to break out of dominant social psychological models of voting in which alignment is seen as produced by an individual-level process of value formation'.

Clearly issue analysis and socialization theory are both incompatible with the consumption cleavage approach to voting behaviour: the first because it brings with it a test which (as we have seen) is not in general passed by the cleavage in question, and the second because it is rejected by the consumption theorists. We will see below that there is a reason for this rejection. Socialization theory provides an alternative explanation for much of what consumption theorists claim for their own approach. Unless they do reject it, they cannot show that different consumption locations represent any more than an as yet unrealized *potential* basis for electoral choice.

However, to point out a contradiction is not to dispose of it. The fact that socialization theory cannot coexist with consumption cleavages as an explanation of current voting behaviour does not tell us which one is wrong.

**How well do consumption cleavages explain voting behaviour?**

One test for a new theory is that it should explain the world at least as well as the theory it seeks to supplant. When applied as an explanation of electoral behaviour, consumption cleavage theory fails this test. The failure is not evident in Dunleavy's presentation, since he focuses on the effects of particular conjunctions of characteristics rather than on the extent to which voting behaviour as a whole is explained by those characteristics. Thus he points out that home-owning households with two cars are 4.39 times more likely to vote Conservative than respondents with no car who rent from a local authority (Dunleavy, 1979, Table 10). This is slightly larger than the largest differences in the chances of voting Conservative between middle-class and working-class social grades (4.12 in the same table). What he fails to point out is that there are relatively few households with two or more cars, compared to the number of middle-class individuals, so the powerful effect only helps us understand a small part of what is to be explained.

If a socialization theorist were to choose the same approach as that employed by Dunleavy, he could demonstrate far more apparently impressive effects. We saw in Figure 1.2 that the chances of voting Conservative among individuals all of whose face-to-face contacts appear to have occurred in working-class contexts was less than one per cent in 1964, while their chances of voting Labour was fully 98 per cent. Even after the reductions in class voting that had occurred by 1979, the corresponding difference in proportions still amounted to over 80 per cent. This represents a difference in chances at least twice as great as that between two-car owning houseowners and carless council tenants. But the comparison is clearly meaningless because of the very small number of such 'ideal type' individuals.

We have no reason to suppose that Dunleavy intended to mislead us with his empirical findings. However, his analysis does mislead because the multivariate technique he employs (known as log-linear modelling) focuses on the *effects* of particular combinations of characteristics, rather than on the extent to which these effects succeed in *explaining* voting behaviour. The difference between these two ways of measuring relationships was briefly outlined at the end of Chapter 1. When, instead of log-linear analysis, the alternative technique of multiple regression is employed, the ability of Housing and Car Ownership to explain voting choice in 1979 does not exceed 12 per cent of variance, whereas the extent of variance explained in voting choice by the six most powerful socialization variables approaches 25 per cent (see below).

There are of course problems involved in comparisons of this kind. One derives from the fact that the socialization variables normally employed in explaining voting choice include measures of childhood home environment (Parents' Party and Parents' Class) which may well overstate the connection between background characteristics and Present Party Preference because of the possibility that respondents 'remember' a class and party background consistent with their present preferences. Error in recall of childhood characteristics is now thought to be slight (see Chapter 3) but might still overstate the influence of childhood home environment. A second problem derives from the fact that there are more socializing variables available for analysis than consumption cleavage variables, with corresponding extra possibilities for explaining variance. One way to overcome this problem is to introduce additional consumption cleavage variables into the analysis, beyond those employed by Dunleavy. For example, we might add Telephone Ownership and Private Medical Insurance to Home Ownership and Car Ownership, giving us four consumption cleavage variables to match the four socializing variables that are left if early home environment is omitted. When the variance explained by these four consumption cleavage variables is compared with that explained by Education and adult socializing variables, the socializing variables still come out ahead, explaining 17 per cent of variance in voting choice compared with 13 per cent by the consumption cleavage variables.

But there is a more fundamental problem inherent in these comparisons. So far we have not recalled the identity of the adult socialization variables. They are of course Occupation, Union Membership, and Housing. As we already know from Chapter 1, the Housing variable plays a major part in our understanding of adult socialization as well as being critical to consumption cleavage theory. In both cases it has been since 1966 the best predictor of partisanship when recalled party preference of parents is omitted. Whether it is interpreted as a socializing variable or as a measure of consumption location is a matter of theory, not data analysis; and so the extent of variance it can explain is not helpful in assessing the relative merits of the two approaches. Consumption cleavage theorists assert that the power of housing to determine partisanship derives from its central position in defining the major political cleavage of the day. Socialization theorists assert that its power derives from the increasing importance of the adult home environment in comparison to childhood or workplace environments. They point out that increasing leisure time and above all increasing stratification of neighbourhoods into homogeneous groups of housing, either privately owned or rented from a local authority, have served to make social contacts around the location of the home a more influential factor than in the past (Rose, 1974). Because of the ambiguous nature of the Home Tenure variable, any critical test of consumption cleavage theory must depend on evaluating the ability of other cleavage variables to explain what socialization variables cannot explain.

Such a test was conducted in the full article from which the present discussion is paraphrased (Franklin and Page, 1984). It showed conclusively that while Car Ownership in particular did add to the variance that could be explained by socialization variables (including Housing) it did not add anything to an explanation that included measures of pro-Labour and pro-Conservative policy evaluations. This finding does not rule out a view that would give primacy to consumption cleavages in structuring attitudes relating to political parties, but merely makes it clear that consumption cleavage theory can only add to the *quality* of an explanation, not to the *extent* of the phenomena that we can explain. It is by way of their impact on issue preferences that the consumption cleavage variables must be operating, if they are having any effect at all.

However, the cleavage variables we have been considering did not go very far towards explaining the extent of pro-Labour and pro-Conservative policy evaluations in 1979. Table 2.3 shows the degree of inter-correlation of these two policy variables with a variety of individual issue preferences as well as with our four cleavage variables. It shows clearly that although Housing, in its usual ambiguous way, does correlate with the two measures of policy preference, neither measure correlates even as well as 0.2 with any other consumption cleavage variable. This is in contrast to considerably more powerful correlations with more conventional issues. The finding is hardly surprising given the low salience in electoral terms of all the consumption cleavage variables.

So consumption cleavage theory does not explain anything that cannot be explained with existing theoretical constructs, and particularly socialization together with issue voting. Moreover, even as a structuring concept which attempts to explain policy preferences on a wide range of issues, it appears to have little to offer.

We do not claim that traditional approaches to explaining voting choice are without fault. Socialization theory, in particular, has often

Table 2.3.  *Inter-correlations (Pearson's r) between issue-based party*
*preferences and cleavage and issue variables, 1979\**

| Cleavage/issue | RPC | RPL | Cleavage/issue | RPC | RPL |
|---|---|---|---|---|---|
| R's home | 0.233 | 0.178 | Any cars | 0.190 | 0.108 |
| Two cars | 0.194 | 0.108 | Med insurance | 0.162 | 0.100 |
| Telephone | 0.133 | 0.086 | | | |
| Abortion | 0.048 | 0.003 | Armament cuts | 0.254 | 0.208 |
| Countryside | 0.032 | 0.056 | Commy threat | 0.136 | 0.136 |
| Comprehensives | 0.412 | 0.383 | EEC policies | 0.228 | 0.186 |
| Foreign aid | 0.112 | 0.115 | Health | 0.136 | 0.109 |
| Immigration | 0.149 | 0.188 | Job creation | 0.396 | 0.364 |
| Land ownership | 0.330 | 0.316 | Nationalization | 0.449 | 0.418 |
| Poor | 0.178 | 0.181 | Pornography | 0.002 | 0.018 |
| Race equality | 0.132 | 0.131 | Race relations | 0.087 | 0.111 |
| Sex equality | 0.114 | 0.097 | Social services | 0.347 | 0.301 |
| Social welfare | 0.341 | 0.300 | Tax vs service | 0.235 | 0.173 |
| Teachers | 0.241 | 0.194 | Trade union law | 0.423 | 0.408 |
| Wages | 0.014 | 0.029 | Wealth | 0.409 | 0.349 |
| Workers | 0.260 | 0.245 | | | |

\* RPC = Respondent pro Conservative on issues
  RPL = Respondent pro Labour on issues

been used as a residual explanation for anything that could be seen as co-determinous with group boundaries. Thus union membership is often presented as though it affected votes through reinforcing existing class influences by bringing together persons with similar class charac-teristics in an additional group context. This mechanism is highly debatable, since it is not clear that union members very often meet as such. Moreover, if this were the mechanism at work, then white-collar union membership should serve to reinforce the predominantly middle-class characteristics of the members of such unions. We shall see in Chapter 3 that this does not happen. Instead, white-collar union members become more likely to vote Labour than white-collar non-union members, just as do their blue-collar counterparts. So union membership clearly operates within a context that is not as blind to policy implications as the socialization approach would have had us believe. And if this is true of union membership, why not of housing? Rather than focusing on the fact that housing does not rank first in most people's estimation of important political concerns, perhaps we should focus instead on the fact that it did rank first for nearly one in ten of 1979 voters. For those people it was an issue as well as a socializing force. For others it may still have been an issue, though of lesser importance; and the number of people affected by housing as an issue may well be growing with the passage of time.

So we would be the last to deny the manifest *potential* of consumption cleavages to structure partisanship should they become more politicized, either through one of the well-understood mechanisms of orthodox political science or through some other mechanism as yet undemonstrated. All we are saying is that the bias (Schattschneider, 1960) inherent in this cleavage seems as yet largely unmobilized. In claiming too much of consumption cleavage theory in the electoral sphere, Dunleavy in particular has been led to discount the validity of the very indicators we need to watch in monitoring the progress of these important developments. We shall have reason to return to the consumption cleavage approach from this perspective when we come to review suggested reasons for the changing basis of British politics, in Chapter 7.

## Summary and implications

In this chapter we have investigated three alternative approaches to the one that was adopted in Chapter 1, for studying the extent and nature of social influences on voting choice. One approach, exemplified by Whiteley and Himmelweit, consists of variations on our own approach, and we saw in the first part of this chapter why these variants would be less appropriate to our present needs. A second approach, exemplified particularly by Rose, ignores the causal order of social processes to focus on the effects of greatest magnitude. The central part of this chapter showed how this approach was poorly adapted to explaining social change. Finally, the third approach, which constitutes the most fundamental challenge to our own, was discussed at length in the last part of the chapter. There we saw how Consumption Cleavage Theory constitutes a challenge not only to our approach but to the whole basis of existing electoral research.

But the major implication of this review has been to rehabilitate socialization theory as describing a viable mechanism for transmitting party allegiance. The attack on the pre-existing orthodoxy mounted by the consumption cleavage theorists is not based on demonstrating its defects as a means of explaining political phenomena, and neither has its proposed replacement been shown superior in this respect. Indeed, quite the contrary. Although the theoretical underpinnings of the model that was presented in Chapter 1 do have weaknesses, these weaknesses do not support the consumption cleavage challenge. So the socialization approach survives to serve as the basis for our further studies. As a first step we must now see how the variables depicted in our model have been affected by social changes over the past twenty years.

# 3
# THE CHANGING SOCIAL CONTEXT OF
# VOTING CHOICE

The variables that we introduced in Chapter 1 as corresponding to the six social characteristics most closely connected with voting choice are not changeless features of the British social landscape. In a changing world social structure changes too, and these variables more than many. Economic growth means more white-collar jobs; greater wealth means more owner-occupied houses and perhaps more children being sent to private schools. Indeed, even jobs that remain manual in nature may no longer have the same socializing effect as increasing mechanization brings fewer opportunities for working closely with others.

But economic growth is only one source of change in British society, and perhaps not so important a source as in many other countries. Other sources of change derive more directly from government policies. A combination of tax advantages for speculative property ownership and legislation protecting tenants rights has had the effect of dramatically reducing the number of people renting their homes from private landlords. A major educational reform aimed at removing the effects of class segregation on disadvantaged children has had the effect of wiping out the distinction between grammer schools and secondary moderns that constituted the basis of British education twenty years ago. Finally, change has come as a result of policies implemented not by governments but by employers and unions, encouraging the extension of union membership among white-collar workers.

There have, of course, been many other sources of change, and many other things have changed in the past twenty years. But already we have covered sources of change to four of our six socializing variables: Education, Occupation, Housing, and Union Membership. The other two, Parents' Class and Parents' Partisanship, will reflect these other changes in due course, as the people affected by educational and social changes become parents in their turn.

In this chapter we will look at each of the six variables that we take to define a person's social context, exploring the extent of change that has occurred since 1964, the reasons for the change, and the

possible consequences for voting choice that might have been anticipated from an understanding of the model presented in Chapter 1. We
will then make a first try at determining the consequences for voting
choice that actually occurred by looking at the evolving relationship
between each variable and voting choice over the same period. After
having dealt with all six variables in this way, we will put the various
changes together and, making the assumption that effects remained
constant, see what changes in electoral support the major parties might
have expected to enjoy on the basis simply of demographic changes in
the number of people with different sets of characteristics. This
exercise will provide us with an expected division of the two-party vote
between 1964 and 1979 based on changes in social structure. Such a
set of expectations can serve as a baseline for comparison with actual
levels of party support in those years, helping us to pin-point changes
that cannot be attributed simply to these aspects of social change.
Because there was little time between the two elections of 1974 for
changes in social characteristics to show themselves, these two elections
are treated together in this chapter, by simply averaging the results
obtained from each sample.

Before we can proceed, however, we must introduce the data upon
which our studies are based, and the surveys from which they derive.

### The surveys employed in this study

Since 1964, each General Election has been closely followed by a
survey of the British electorate conducted by a team of social scientists
anxious to unravel the true nature of the political choice that the
nation had just made. These surveys were funded by the British
Economic and Social Research Council, and were conducted first by
researchers at the University of Oxford (David Butler and Donald
Stokes) in 1964, 1966, and 1970, and then by researchers at the
University of Essex (Ivor Crewe, Bo Sarlvik, James Alt, and David
Robertson) in 1974 and 1979. At the time of writing a survey is again
in the field, this time directed by Anthony Heath of the University of
Oxford, to study the election of 1983. Except for the last of these,
which will not be available to scholars such as myself until 1985, all
the data collected in these studies have been made available for analysis
by other scholars through the ESRC Data Archive at the University of
Essex. The number of people interviewed was never less than 1,700.

Two other surveys were conducted as part of this sequence, but not following any General Election, in 1963 and 1969. These had an important part to play in unravelling the nature of public opinion between elections, but have little to offer the present study. Occasionally we make use of questions asked in 1963 of individuals who were reinterviewed in 1964 when the same questions were not asked. We make no use of the 1969 study.

Each of these surveys formed part of a larger whole, for each established a panel of voters who could be re-interviewed after the next election. (In 1966 and October 1974 no new panel was established following a short Parliament, and the same panel was reinterviewed a third time following the next election.) We make little use of the panel element of the various election studies in this book, although occasionally it is very helpful for us to be able to check on responses to an earlier interview in order to be able to establish who changed their party support from one election to the next, or to measure the extent of social mobility. Nor do we employ very many of the hundreds of variables that were collected in the course of the studies. We make most use of Voting Choice, and of the six social structure variables represented in the model we outlined in Chapter 1. In addition we employ in later chapters measures of party identification and a number of issue-related variables. As already stated, this book is not a comprehensive study of British voting behaviour. It is an attempt to trace the evolution of one important component in voting choice (social class) in order to establish how class used to affect voting choice, what changes in this effect have taken place, and what the consequences of these changes have been. For these purposes only a small number of variables were relevant, of which the most important are discussed in this chapter.

We do employ one other survey not included in this set of academic election studies, in order to extend our coverage to include the election of 1983. Since the academic study of this election will not be available until after this book is in press we employ a Gallup survey conducted before and during polling and directed by Ivor Crewe. This is an impressive study including many issue variables and involving over four thousand respondents. However, for our purposes it is badly flawed because it contains no measures of childhood characteristics (not even education), and other variables are often measured somewhat differently than in the academic surveys. So in what follows we employ the Gallup study with caution and only in so far as findings are consistent with trends established in earlier studies.

In the sections that follow, at the same time as we describe changes in social structure occurring in the past twenty years, we also discuss different ways of measuring these changes, and in the process introduce some of the variables to be employed in our analyses. Many of these variables leave a great deal to be desired as measures of the characteristics concerned, but they were the best means that could be devised of indexing the changes that had occurred during our period. The various compromises made in measuring different variables were embodied in rules for recoding the variables already present in our surveys. Deciding on appropriate rules was made even more difficult by our need to maximize comparability in our measures of class characteristics from survey to survey.

Many of the variables we employ are imperfect because of missing data arising from respondents who would not or could not answer one question or another. Sometimes the proportions of missing data varied so much from election to election for particular variables that the only way of obtaining reasonably consistent measurements of the characteristics over time was to lump together all respondents who did not report having a certain characteristic, whether or not they told us anything at all relating to the variable concerned. To take education as an example, everyone who did not report having stayed at school after the age of 16 was assumed to have left school by that age, whether or not we had any indication of the actual age at which they left school (coding of the Education variable is further discussed below). Other variables are imperfect because the measure we would have preferred, even if it was available in some of the studies, was not available in all of them. Thus we could not measure the impact of union membership by seeing whether or not there was a union member in each household, because this question was not always asked in the same form in different surveys. Instead we measure union membership according to whether or not respondents were themselves members of a union.

The precise manner in which each variable is measured for each election studied is detailed in an appendix to this book. All variables relating to social circumstances are coded 1 for persons who have an attribute of interest to us (a working class occupation, perhaps, or Labour-voting parents) and 0 for those who do not have the attribute in question. In every case the choice of attribute to code as 1 for any variable was determined by the impact of the variable on *Labour* voting. Thus if we were looking at council tenants versus others, council tenants would be coded 1 on the housing variable, while others were coded 0; but if we were looking at home-owners versus others, the home-owners would be coded 0 (the category least associated with Labour voting) and the others 1. The appendix describes some important features of such variables which are alluded to in this chapter. The reason for coding the variables so that the positive score matches Labour tendencies is to yield positive effects when predicting Labour votes. When class voting was at its height in 1964, social circumstances predicted Labour voting better than Conservative voting. So predictions of Labour voting are generally the ones we employ in this book. Some further considerations relevant to coding are discussed in the appendix.

## Education

Two developments in British education since 1964 have served to change radically the environment in which most children go to school. The first of these was the virtual abolition of secondary modern and grammar schools, and their replacement by comprehensives. The second was the raising of the school leaving age from 15 to 16 (cf. Cogan, 1978). The transformation of the tertiary education system that also occurred in this period affected too few people to have had any chance of explaining party choice in general, and we ignore the effects of tertiary education in this book.

The Labour Party came to power in 1964 with a commitment to replace the existing dual system of state schools with a single state system that would provide education for all ranges of ability within a single school. There were many reasons for the change, but an important one was the desire to provide all pupils with an environment in which they would be encouraged to develop their abilities equally and to the maximum.

Whether the change in the system of education that came about over the next fifteen years had the desired effect or not, it was almost bound to have other effects that might not have been anticipated. In particular, if Butler and Stokes were right about the effect of the school environment in reinforcing the class effects of early upbringing, then any change in the school environment could have had far-reaching consequences for political socialization. Thus the provision of school environments where some children from working-class households would mix with middle-class children on a regular basis could have diluted the politically socializing effect of the home for these children, and made them less likely to grow up as Labour supporters than under the old system. Alternatively, the middle-class children now being educated in a more working-class environment might have been more fundamentally affected. It would be impossible to tell in advance which party would benefit from any resulting change, but it would be reasonable to suppose that greater mixing of social classes in secondary schools would have the effect of reducing the influence of education on voting choice and ultimately, perhaps, of reducing the influence of class in general.

In fact, reforms of this kind take a long time to bear fruit that is measureable in the electorate as a whole. Although by 1979 there were few children any longer being educated under the old system, the number of adults in our sample who had received a grammar school education (19 per cent) was actually greater than in 1964 (14 per cent). This strange finding derives from the fact that the grammar and secondary modern school system was itself only introduced gradually in the wake of the 1944 Education Act, and its full effects had not been felt on the adult population by the time it was abolished. We cannot measure changes in the number of adults who had received a secondary modern education because they were not distinguished from those who had received other forms of non-selective state education in any of our surveys before 1974. However, the proportion of our samples in grammar school education rose to a peak of 19.5 per cent in 1974, as the increasing intakes of earlier years reached voting age, before the numbers of children entering the electorate from the new comprehensive schools was sufficient to offset this.

Even had the change taken effect more rapidly, it does not seem likely that it would have had any significant impact on partisanship. Those who, in our 1979 sample, had gained their education in the new comprehensive system were no less likely to support the Labour party than their counterparts with a secondary modern or equivalent education. Indeed the proportion of Labour voters among those with a comprehensive education was higher at 52 per cent than the proportion of Labour voters among those with a secondary modern or equivalent education (44 per cent − see Table 3.1).

We saw in Chapter 1 that education is not accorded a direct link with voting choice in the model we presented there. Alone of all the variables included in the model, its effects were felt only indirectly. Direct links between Education and Voting Choice were considered when the model was being developed, but were eliminated because they added little to the variance in voting behaviour that could be explained without them (see Chapter 5). So the apparent influence of Education measured by Butler and Stokes seems in fact to have been largely due to the ability of this variable to represent the impact of other influences, as a sort of stand-in for effects occuring after childhood that these authors did not take into simultaneous account. Indeed, given the close links with R's Occupation that were illustrated in the model, it seems likely that R's Education was serving as something of a surrogate for this variable in particular.

Table 3.1. *Proportion of Labour voters among respondents having attended different types of schools, 1979*

| Type of school attended | Proportion voting Lab | Grouped proportions voting Lab | Ns. |
|---|---|---|---|
| Grammar, secondary grammar, etc. | 0.248 | 0.248 | 321 |
| Comprehensive | 0.522 | | |
| Secondary modern, elementary, etc. | 0.443 | | |
| Commercial, private, etc. | 0.291 | 0.413 | 1,237 |
| Non-selective convent | 0.261 | | |
| Public school | 0.125 | | |

If this view of the role of education is correct, then any change in its influence would only be mirroring the decline of other influences, rather than serving as a prime cause in its own right. However, there is one other development in the realm of educational characteristics that deserves our attention. This is the gradual increase, over the whole of our period, of the average age at which our respondents report having completed their full-time education.

If the importance of education lies not, as Butler and Stokes supposed, in the socializing effect of time spent in proximity with children from a distinctive class background, then it must lie far more prosaicly in the ability of education to provide the skills and abilities required for middle-class occupations. In this case, the important educational distinction between individuals will lie not so much in the nature of the school they attended, as in how long they stayed and what skills they learned. As a crude means of identifying those who took more than a minimal level of skill with them on leaving, all our surveys ask respondents to indicate the age at which they left school, or terminated full-time education.[1] As Table 3.2 indicates, the proportion of our samples reporting having left school before the age of 16 dropped steadily over our period, from over 80 per cent in 1964 to 63 per cent in 1979.

Table 3.2.  *Proportion of respondents leaving school by the age of 16 and 17, 1964 to 1979\**

| Election year | %<br>Left by 16 | %<br>Left by 17 |
|---|---|---|
| 1964 | 80.5 | 90.7 |
| 1966 | 78.8 | 90.0 |
| 1970 | 75.7 | 88.5 |
| 1974* | 72.9 | 86.3 |
| 1979 | 63.7 | 83.2 |

\* 1974 value measured from the February sample.

Quite what effect on class voting should be anticipated from this educational revolution depends on the other characteristics of those staying longer at school. If those who stay longer are predominantly middle class in other respects then the change should have the effect of reinforcing class influences, whereas the reverse would be the case if they were predominantly working class. In either case the development should be expected to benefit the Conservative party over the passage of time, as increasing numbers of voters gain skills associated with

[1] On the basis of these questions it is possible to dichotomize our respondents into those who left school at the earliest possible age and those who voluntarily stayed on after the legal minimum leaving age. This distinction is not always quite as simple to make as might appear, since the school-leaving age has itself been changed twice within the lifetime of many of our respondents, and three times within the memory of some of them, the most recent increases being to 15 in the 1940s and to 16 in the 1970s (see Chapter 1). Nevertheless, by having regard to each respondent's date of birth and the school-leaving age obtaining at the time they would have reached that age, it is possible to distinguish between those who left at the minimum legal age and those who stayed on beyond that time. This dichotomy does not, however, relate as well to voting choice as the simpler distinction between leaving by the age of 16, or staying at school after that age. This is because a large number of respondents, old enough to have left school when the minimum age was less than sixteen, nevertheless stayed on at school longer than they need have done. Most of these had, however, left by the age of sixteen without having gained educational qualifications appropriate to a middle-class occupation. So the concept of educational attainment that we employ in this book is the simpler of the two, distinguishing those who received full time education after the age of 16 from those who did not.

Conservative voting. The link between Parental Class and Extent of Education did increase, if anything, over the period: rising from 0.352 to 0.357 between 1964 and 1974, and remaining fairly constant thereafter (see Chapter 5). So we might have expected the link between Education and Voting Choice also to increase. In fact, as shown in Table 3.2, the link in terms of correlation has, if anything, declined marginally; though it was not very strong in the first place. So despite extensive changes in our educational system, and in the extent to which members of our samples have benefited from it, the resulting consequences for voting choice were probably not great.

## Occupation and union membership

The increasing educational attainments of the British voting population are matched in an unsurprising way by the increase in white-collar occupations that has occurred in the past twenty years. Because of the large number of housewives in our samples, we will follow standard practice in focusing on the occupations of heads of households. By this measure working-class employment has declined progressively since 1964, from 61 per cent of our sample in that year to only 49 per cent of our sample in 1979 (see Table 3.3). The consequences that might have been anticipated from this development depend again on how it is regarded. On the one hand, it might be expected that penetration into

Table 3.3.   *Changing influence of occupation and union membership, 1964–79*

|  | 1964 | 1966 | 1970 | 1974 | 1979 |
|---|---|---|---|---|---|
| Proportion in working-class occupations | 0.607 | 0.618 | 0.592 | 0.521 | 0.492 |
| Correlation with Labour voting | 0.407 | 0.414 | 0.144 | 0.249 | 0.212 |
| Proportion members of unions | 0.233 | 0.247 | 0.242 | 0.273 | 0.302 |
| Correlation with Labour voting | 0.200 | 0.184 | 0.172 | 0.172 | 0.154 |

middle-class occupations of otherwise working-class individuals would cause the middle class to become less Conservative, thus reducing the extent of class voting in such a way as to benefit the Labour party. On the other hand, if these individuals were seduced by middle-class values into adopting a party allegiance consistent with their new occupational status then class voting might remain unchanged, to the benefit of the Tories. No scenario based only on occupational developments would lead us to expect a diminution of Labour party support in the ranks of those remaining in working class occupations, but this is precisely what occurred in practice, as we shall see in Chapter 4. As shown in Table 3.3, the correlation between Occupation and Labour voting declined in fits and starts from 0.407 in 1964 to 0.212 in 1979, indicating that one consequence of increasing social mobility was apparently to reduce the effects of occupation. But to the extent that a relationship between occupation and voting still remains, increasing numbers in middle-class occupations must mean increasing numbers of Tory voters.

Turning to union membership, trends over the period were again such as to confound a priori expectations. The traditional association between the unions and working-class occupations would have led one to expect a reduction of unionization as the proportion of working-class individuals declined. In fact any such potential decline was more than offset by a recruiting drive that extended far into traditionally middle-class occupations such as the Civil Service, teaching, and lecturing; and Table 3.3 shows that the proportion of respondents reporting membership in a labour union increased from under a quarter to about a third during the past twenty years. In turn, such a transformation of the union movement might have been expected to dilute the impact of union membership on partisanship. If unionization was supposed to reinforce other class characteristics by bringing class members into contact with other members of their class, then a middle-class union should have reinforced middle class characteristics with the result that union membership itself would cease to have so strong a link with partisanship. Superficially, this appears to have happened to some extent. Table 3.3 shows the correlation between Union Membership and Voting Choice to have declined by almost a quarter over the period. But we will see below that this uncontrolled relationship understates the impact of the variable, which has in fact increased its importance when other effects are held constant. This implies that the power of union membership to reinforce other influences on partisanship was based on more than face-to-face contact among people with similar occupational characteristics. Apparently the effect of union membership is to inculcate working-class values even on otherwise middle-class individuals, and this is the effect that was illustrated in our model of class voting. This being the case, the developments in union membership since 1964 will have been to the electoral advantage of the Labour party.

### Housing

It is changes in the pattern of housing tenure that have aroused the most theoretical interest of all the developments we need to consider. These changes have been threefold. In the first place, increasing affluence has enabled more individuals to purchase their own houses, either directly or (more usually) on a mortgage. The stock of owner-occupied housing rose from 42 per cent in 1960 to 50 per cent in 1970 (Butler and Sloman, 1979), and 54 per cent in 1977. In the second place, the number of dwellings built and rented by local authorities also increased from 26 per cent in 1960 to 32 per cent in 1977. This means, most importantly, that the stock of other housing (mostly rented from private landlords) declined during this period from 32 per cent in 1960 to only 14 per cent in 1977 (see Figure 3.1).

These trends, significant in the case of private and local authority housing stock and striking in the case of private rented housing, can be regarded in two different ways depending on whether stress is placed on

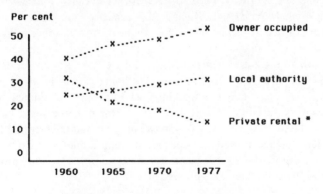

\* Includes other forms of tenure until 1970.

Figure 3.1.   Housing tenancy in Britain, 1960–77.
*Source*: Butler and Sloman, *British Political Facts.*

the socializing influence of housing or its role in structuring a potential social cleavage. If attention is focused on the potential of the home environment to reinforce class influences by bringing people into contact with others who have similar social characteristics, then the decline of the privately-rented housing market and progressive concentration of individuals into middle-class or working-class ghettos (see Chapter 1) should be to increase the influence of housing in determining partisanship.[2]

Alternatively, housing can be looked at in terms of the economic interests that distinguish owner-occupiers from council tenants. The latter are dependent on the state for provision of the most important item of consumption in their lives (housing) while the former make private provision for this service. We saw in Chapter 2 that, in the view of Patrick Dunleavy and other researchers, this gives rise to a consumption cleavage in which the interests of one group are different from those of the other. This cleavage might be reinforced by other similar cleavages between those who depend on the state for provision of services such as transport, education, and health, and those who make private provision, as already discussed.

From the point of view of our present concerns the important thing about these two approaches is that they give rise to similar expectations: that the importance of housing in determining voting choice should have increased since 1964. In fact, this has not happened, as demonstrated in Table 3.4 which shows the uncontrolled correlation between Housing and Voting Choice to have in fact declined somewhat over the period. However, an influence that remains more or less constant may be viewed as increasing in importance relative to other influences which are declining, as we shall see in the final section of this chapter. Meanwhile, the consequences of these changes for party choice depend on whether the middle-class influences of home ownership are felt more or less strongly than the working-class influences of council house tenancy. In fact both of these influences rose over the years; but the greater number of individuals in private housing, and the fact that twice as many people moved into private housing as moved into council housing during the period, yielded a balance in favour of the Conservatives as these developments proceeded.

---

[2] This assumes that the growth of home-ownership is greater among otherwise middle-class groups than among otherwise working-class groups, and vice versa for the growth in council tenancies.

Table 3.4.   *Changing influence of housing tenure, 1964-1979*

|  | 1964 | 1966 | 1970 | 1974 | 1979 |
|---|---|---|---|---|---|
| Proportion not in owner-occupied housing | 0.533 | 0.534 | 0.496 | 0.466 | 0.430 |
| Correlation with Labour voting | 0.322 | 0.296 | 0.130 | 0.253 | 0.237 |

## Parental class and partisanship

The number of working-class parents reflects the number of working-class individuals in earlier years. So declining numbers of working-class individuals will in due course lead to declining numbers of working-class parents, and the same thing will happen in the case of preferences for any particular political party. Similarly, links between these characteristics and the partisanship of children can be expected to decline as children for whom social chaaracteristics are less important determinants of voting choice become parents in their turn.

Of course there are problems of measurement involved in estimating the effects of parental class and party on the partisanship of British voters. In our surveys we depend on respondents to tell us about the class and partisanship of their parents, and these are characteristics that might easily have been misremembered, perhaps in such a way as to bring them into line with perceptions of a respondent's own present circumstances. Past voting is notoriously subject to recall error, as strikingly documented in recent research (Katz, Niemi, and Newman, 1980), so why should not parental characteristics be equally subject to bias in our samples?

In fact there is good reason to believe that childhood characteristics are not subject to the kind of recall error that bedevils the study of past voting choice. Other research has shown that recall of parents' partisanship is very good (Dowse and Hughes, 1971; Jennings and Niemi, 1981) and we can ourselves carry out a simple test to discover whether present circumstances bias recall of childhood class environment. If respondents were to misremember childhood influences to bring them into line with current perceptions, then any change in current perceptions should be reflected in some change in perceived childhood influences. Given that some of our respondents were asked more than once about childhood characteristics, in successive waves of our panel studies, we can match up changes in present circumstances with changes in recalled childhood characteristics. Between 1963 and 1966, for example, only 55 per cent of respondents to the Oxford studies gave consistant and unchanging responses to questions on childhood class and present party identification (parents party was not asked again in 1966), but only half of one per cent changed both responses in such a way as to keep them consistent; and the correlation between change in perception of Childhood Class and change in Current Party Identification was -0.076. Small negative relationships were also obtained between change in Childhood Class and change in Current Social Class. So the evidence is strong that present circumstances do not bias recall of childhood characteristics.

Childhood characteristics (and particularly Parents' Party) are the most powerful determinants of voting choice, and movement in these characteristics reflects changes in social structure and voting alignment of a generation ago. So recent developments in social structure (which we have seen in past sections to have been generally likely to have benefited the Conservatives) might well be vitiated by changes that occurred many years before. In particular, the rise in Labour voting to a peak in 1945 must have had an impact on the next generation rising to a peak sometime during the following twenty to forty years: precisely the period covered by our study.

In fact, changes in parents' class in the past twenty years have been quite different from changes in Parents Party. The latter has moved (as expected) in a Labour direction since 1964, with increasing numbers of respondents reporting Labour-voting parents as time went on. This movement has completely overshadowed the much more gradual movement of Parents' Class in a middle-class direction, as shown in Table 3.5. The result of these trends should have been to the benefit of the Labour party, reaping the rewards of parenthood among its converts of earlier years; and indeed this has probably been the effect. While the correlation between Parents' Party and Respondent's Partisanship has declined, this has only been by about 10 per cent of its 1964 extent (0.325, see Table 3.5). By contrast, the number of Labour-voting parents increased by over a third in the same period. Parents' Party remains today easily the most powerful predictor of partisanship, yielding a correlation of 0.319 with Voting Choice, as also shown in the same table.

It is important to note that throughout this book we count Parents' Party as a *class* characteristic. One justification for this has already been given in Chapter 1: Parents' Party is a variable that largely reflects and

Table 3.5. *Changing influence of parents' party and parents' class, 1964-1979*

|  | 1964 | 1966 | 1970 | 1974 | 1979 |
|---|---|---|---|---|---|
| Proportion with Labour-voting parents | 0.303 | 0.311 | 0.391 | 0.395 | 0.419 |
| Correlation with Labour voting | 0.350 | 0.368 | 0.288 | 0.293 | 0.319 |
| Proportion with working-class parents | 0.768 | 0.771 | 0.752 | 0.736 | 0.731 |
| Correlation with Labour voting | 0.261 | 0.275 | 0.222 | 0.201 | 0.202 |

reinforces the influence of the early home environment. But more importantly, this conflation of party with class in the case of parents (not, of course, in the case of our respondents themselves) is a convenience that permits us to avoid many cumbersome phrases in the remainder of the book.

## Estimating the effects of social change

In previous sections we have speculated about the consequences of change in each variable taken individually. But all the social characteristics have been changing at the same time, some in a direction that might have been expected to benefit one major party and some in a direction that might have been expected to benefit the other. So the speculations we have engaged in have been largely idle ones, except in so far as they may have helped bring to life the underlying mechanics of change.

In order to really assess the likely consequences of the social changes we have enumerated we have to apply them to the effects depicted in the model that was presented in Chapter 1, so as to reach a conclusion about the likely outcome *on balance* of all the changes we have discussed. To do this we treat that model in terms of the primary regression equation from which it was developed (see Chapter 5). This derives from a prediction of voting choice in 1964 based on all the structural variables in that model, including education. The coefficients in question have already been illustrated in Figure 1.2 and will be displayed for other purposes in Figure 3.4 below. The nature of the analysis from which they derive was already explored in the central sections of Chapter 2.

One feature of the effects computed in such an analysis is that when average values of each of the explanatory variables included in it are entered into the resulting equation, the prediction that emerges is of the average value of the variable being explained. In this case, the average values of explanatory variables correspond to the proportions having each social characteristic, and the average value of the variable being explained is the proportion voting Labour in 1964. So if the proportions of voters having each characteristic in 1964 are multiplied by the corresponding coefficients and the results are summed, the result will, by definition, be the Labour vote for 1964.

When the proportions of our samples having each social characteristic in *subsequent* years are entered into the *same* equation (the one computed for 1964), the outcome yields an *expected* Labour vote for each of those subsequent years based uniquely on changes in social structure. This is no more than an accounting operation similar to adding up an electricity bill for consumption of units priced differently for different times of day, where the different tarrifs are artificially held constant over time. In such a case, changes in the total expected electricity bill would be due solely to changes in consumption and not to price increases. In dealing with political change, the analogue for changes in consumption is changes in social structure, while changes in price would be analageous to changes in the nature of the forces depicted in Figure 1.1. It is these that we wish to hold constant.

It is true that if we hold constant the forces depicted in Figure 1.1, this is tantamount to assuming that there had been no decline in class voting. Since this is a book about exactly that decline, the assumption is likely to turn out to be unwarranted. However, the calculation can tell us what would have been the movement in electoral forces resulting from changes in social structure had there not been any decline in class voting, or any other changes in effects on voting behaviour over the period of our study.

## Social change and Labour voting

Figure 3.2 shows (broken line) the expected percentage voting Labour out of all votes cast in the elections of 1964 to 1979, assuming the social determinants of voting measured in 1964 and illustrated in Figure 1.1

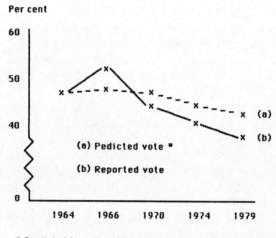

Figure 3.2. Predictions for Labour voting from changing social
characteristics, compared with reported Labour voting,
1964–79

to have been the only important ones, and moreover to have remained unchanged in extent in subsequent elections. So the broken line shows the changes in Labour strength that would have resulted from the social changes that have been the subject of this chapter, all other things being equal. Because social characteristics had no time to show significant changes between the two elections of 1974, these two surveys are again treated together in the illustration, and in the discussions that follow. The projection could not be continued to 1983 because our survey of that election does not contain many of the variables from which the calculations are made.

Other things have indeed not been equal. As we shall demonstrate particularly in Chapter 6, election results are not only determined by social characteristics. Moreover, the extent of the effects of particular social characteristics have also changed, as already noted and as we shall demonstrate particularly in Chapters 4 and 5. So the changes in Labour voting strength reported by our respondents to successive surveys (solid line) do not match the predictions. Nor does reported Labour voting amongst these respondents accurately match the actual pro- portion of votes cast for the Labour party in each election, which is generally less than the reported percentage.[3] The match is particularly poor in 1966, but this prediction (and the reported proportion voting Labour) should probably not be given too much credence, since no new sample was drawn for this election. Instead the panel started in 1963 was 'topped up' with new respondents to replace those lost through attrition during the intervening years. The result is not a proper cross-section of the electorate since both the very old and the very young were under-represented, as were those with particularly high geographic mobility. Moreover, the newly added respondents were not asked certain questions that had been asked of other respondents in 1964 (particularly about their housing and union membership) so that these variables (a third of those used in our prediction) will be particularly susceptible to bias.

Nevertheless, Figure 3.2 is remarkable in displaying a prediction that always moves in the same direction as reported voting choice. If we had known nothing more about the determinants of voting choice than was depicted in Figure 1.1, we would have been able to anticipate a large part of the decline in Labour voting that occurred after 1970 purely on the basis of the changing social conditions that have been the subject of the present chapter. These would not have enabled us to anticipate the increased Labour majority of 1966, nor the Tory victory of 1970; but the general pattern of Labour voting over the ensuing ten years would have come as no surprise.

The ability to anticipate changes in party support on the basis of changes in social structure is important for two reasons. In the first place it provides a demonstration of the utility of the causal modelling exercise conducted in Chapter 1. The model depicted in Figure 1.1 purported to illustrate the causal connections between social character-istics and voting choice. It implied that changes in those characteristics on the part of individuals would lead to change in their voting choices, and that changes in the social-structure of the whole society would similarly be reflected in the voting choice of the society taken as a whole. But causal connections were not ascertained by looking at the way in which votes changed in response to changing conditions. To be able to derive the model in that way would have required a series of massive social experiments in which individuals were moved from one

---

[3] Sarlvik and Crewe (1983, p. 346) explain how a 'bandwaggon effect' in favour of the victorious party usually biases recall of recent voting decisions, so that (for example) in 1979 the reported Conservative vote was 2.1 per cent in excess of that actually cast.

social background to another, from one job to another, and so forth. Such a set of experiments would have been impracticable and probably not decisive in establishing the nature of causal processes, since the human beings involved could hardly be unaffected by the fact that they were being experimented upon.

So the model was derived instead from what is often called a 'quasi-experiment' in which variance in the explanatory variables derives not from manipulating them directly but from making use of such variation as occurs naturally in the course of events. Some people responding to our surveys had been brought up in one kind of environment and some in another, some had one kind of occupation and some another, and so forth. These differences provided us with the variability we could not get from experiments, and the opportunity to explain this variability by means of social factors. This procedure was treated in Chapter 1 as purely heuristic. The model was a device that helped us understand the world. Figure 3.2, however, shows that the model also has practical uses, more of which will become evident in Chapter 5.[4]

The second important thing about our ability to project expected voting choice forward through time on the basis of changing social structure lies precisely in the fact that Figure 3.2 does *not* show our predictions according precisely with actually observed voting choices. To the extent that it shows the world behaving other than might have been anticipated from our model, it focuses attention on those changes that remain in most need of explanation. In particular, it focuses attention on the elections of 1966 and 1970 that produced changes in voting choice far greater than can be explained by changes in social structure during that period. The 1966 deviation need not perhaps be taken too seriously. The sample is defective, as already noted, and the

---

[4] Of course, the changes we are looking at in Figure 3.2 are changes pertaining to *society as a whole* while the model depicted in Figure 1.1 was a model of *individual* voting choice. Nevertheless, the model was based on an analysis of individuals most of whom entered the electorate with the characteristics they reported in our survey. Relatively few will have been reporting characteristics newly acquired as a consequence of changes in their own circumstances. So general changes are the only ones the model can be expected to reflect. Nevertheless, even had there been total conformity between predicted and actual electoral change, this would not imply that there had been no developments in the nature of individual voting choice: merely that any such developments did not affect the overall balance of party support. The analysis in this section constitutes what is technically known as an 'ecological' analysis because it relates to individuals in general rather than in particular. Ecological analyses can often be misleading in their implications as to behaviour at the level of the individual, as we shall have reason to point out again in Chapters 5 and 6.

swing to Labour that occurred in 1966 was partly due to changes among those who had not voted either Conservative or Labour in 1964, and whose behaviour is not predicted by our analysis (see below). The 1970 deviation, however, is critical. Between 1966 and 1970 Labour voting dropped by almost exactly 5 per cent (Figure 3.2 makes the decline look nearer 10 per cent because it so badly misrepresents the Labour vote in 1966). Changes in social characteristics during the same period would not have led us to anticipate a decline of more than half a percentage point: one tenth of what actually occurred. Just as importantly, the illustration focuses attention away from more recent changes in Labour voting. From 1970 onwards the pattern of Labour voting followed somewhat more closely the expectations that derive from our model of voting choice applied to changing social characteristics since that date. Almost half of the decline in Labour voting from then until 1979 followed naturally from changing social structure in those ten years.

### Social change and Conservative voting

The story, however, is rather different for the Conservatives. For if, given the relationships between social characteristics that existed in 1964, the developments in social structure discussed in this chapter constituted a liability for the Labour Party, those same changes constituted a bonanza for the Conservative Party. In 1964, only some 12 per cent of the electorate voted other than Labour or Tory. Had minor party voting not changed in subsequent elections, then the Conservatives would have stood to gain what the Labour party lost. On the basis of the model depicted in Figure 1.1 the expected Conservative vote should have risen precisely to reflect the decline in the Labour vote. In fact Figure 3.3 shows the story to be more complex. In 1974 the Conservatives lost votes instead of gaining them, but in 1979 they won back the position that would have been expected on the basis of changing social structure.

In this illustration there are again two results that do not accord with expectations. However, for the Conservative party these results occurred not in 1966 and 1970 but in 1970 and 1974. In the first of these elections they did better than expected, reciprocating Labour's loss in the same election, but instead of them moving in parallel with expectations derived from changing social structure as the Labour vote then did, the Tory vote suffered an unexpected loss in February

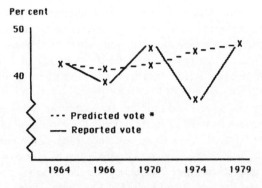

* Predicted from the 1964 regression analysis employing
the six social characteristics discussed in this chapter.

Figure 3.3.    Predictions* for Conservative voting from changing
social circumstances compared with reported Conservative
voting, 1964–79

1974 which was accentuated in the October election of that year, from
which they recovered five years later. It is noteworthy that 1966 does
not constitute as much of an anomalous result for the Tories as it did
for Labour (Figure 3.2), and also that 1974 *does* constitute an anomalous result for the Tories though it was not an anomalous result for
Labour. These contrasting patterns in Figure 3.2 and 3.3 show that the
results for 1966 and 1974 partially reflect movements in and out of
major party voting, either from abstention or from minor party voting,
which are simply not addressed by our model of voting choice as
initially defined (these considerations will be addressed in Chapter 4).
They thus do not constitute failures of prediction of the same kind as
that which occurs in 1970.

### The status of the projections

These projections of 1964 voting behaviour based on changing social
conditions through the following fifteen years leave us with two questions to ponder. What accounts for variations in the extent of major
party voting (such as benefited Labour in 1966 and hurt the Tories in
1974); and what was it about 1970 that caused such a radical swing in
electoral fortunes from one major party to the other? We will address
these questions in later chapters. However, one preliminary matter must

be dealt with now. This is the question of whether the exercise conducted in this section is a reasonable one. We stated at the outset that
we were making the unrealistic assumption that the effects of social
structure remained constant even while the structure itself was in a
state of flux. How unrealistic was that assumption, and what difference
does it make if we relax it?

Figure 3.4 shows the assumption to have been very unrealistic
indeed, and the effects of different variables to have been in an even
greater state of flux than the social structure to which they relate. We
do indeed begin and end our period with effect coefficients of very
comparable magnitude for all but one of the six variables. The effects
of Parents' Class, Parents' Party, Extent of Education, Type of Housing,
and Union Membership are virtually identical in 1979 to their values
fifteen years earlier. Only the effect of Occupation drops by more than
5 percentage points, and its decline is indeed more than three times as
great as that. The effect of Parents' Class is down by a third after
recovering somewhat from a low point in 1974, which is something we
will have reason to refer to in later chapters, but the reduction is in an
effect that was already small. So the overwhelming impression is one of
consistency until we look at the elections intervening between 1964
and 1979. In these we see a tremendous amount of movement in the

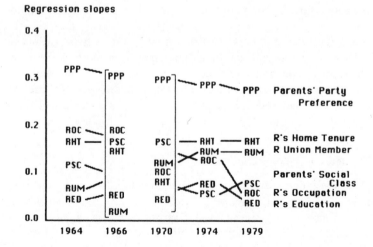

Figure 3.4.   Partial effects on Labour voting of six social characteristics
taken simultaneously as regression predictors, 1964–79

effects of different variables. Indeed, the long term decline in the effect of Occupation appears positively modest in comparison with the wild oscillations in the effects of Parents' Class and Type of Housing. Only the effect of Parents' Party appears relatively unaffected by these swings, declining gently but perceptibly over the period of our concern.

On the face of it, these changes in the importance of individual variables make nonsense of our projections of the expected effects of changing social conditions. The effects of individual variables are clearly much disturbed by features of particular election campaigns. In the next chapter we will gain some feeling for the biases inherent in specific election outcomes, and the ways in which these biases can affect apparent relationships between variables quite unrelated to those really involved. There and in Chapter 5 we will be concerned to develop perspectives on electoral choice that enable us to see the continuities inherent in successive election results even through the smoke-screen thrown up by features peculiar to each. Meanwhile we already know 1970 to have been a deviant election, in need of explanations other than those that can be provided by changing social circumstances; and we also know that 1966 produced a bad sample. If those two sets of coefficients are ignored (they are distinguished in the illustration by being enclosed in square brackets) then the trends shown in Figure 3.4 appear much less volatile. Three variables show a downward trend in their effects: in order of magnitude of the decline these are firstly Occupation then Parents' Party, and finally Parents' Class. One variable shows an upward trend: Union Membership. Two variables show relatively unchanging effects: Housing and Education (although the latter does alternate with Parents' Class in 1974). Moreover, in terms of magnitudes of change, only Occupation shows any appreciable decline, as already observed. So the effect of ignoring coefficients derived from studies of the elections of 1966 and 1970 is to yield a set of effects that do not differ greatly from election to election. Recalculating predicted Labour vote for 1964 to 1979 on the basis of revised coefficients derived from analysis of data from 1974 and 1979 does in fact yield results that follow closely the path taken by predictions based on 1964 coefficients.

Thus the volatility of coefficients displayed in Figure 3.4 does not invalidate the thrust of the argument presented in this section. Except for coefficients computed from studies of the elections of 1966 (biased) and 1970 (deviant), all available estimates of the effects of social structure yield similar estimates of expected division of the major

party vote between 1964 and 1979. What remains to be explained are
the two major deviations shown in Figures 3.2 and 3.3 between the
expected and actual support for major parties: the swing to the Conservatives in 1970, and the rise of minor parties in 1974. In the next
two chapters we will argue that both these events can be traced to a
decline in class voting that occurred between 1966 and 1970. We will
see in Chapter 4 that it was defections among solid working-class erstwhile Labour supporters that provided Conservatives with their victory
in 1970, while Chapter 5 will show how the decline in class voting
inherent in these defections also provided the preconditions for a rise of
minor party voting in the next election. When this view of the political
events of the decade has been established we will still be left with the
task of explaining the decline of class voting, and that will prove far
more intractable. But that will be a problem for subsequent chapters.

## Was the decline of Labour voting inevitable?

There is some risk that the analysis presented in the previous section
will be taken to imply that a decline in Labour voting in the 1970s was
inevitable given the changes in social structure that took place during
the decade. Such an interpretation of our findings is not warranted. The
ability to project events that actually occur does not prove that they
were inevitable. If the courses of two ships are projected, the projection
may show that they will collide. The fact that they then collide does
not prove that nothing could have been done about it; merely that
nothing *was* done about it. There may indeed turn out to be reasons
why nothing was done (the steering mechanisms of both ships jammed,
the duty watch of both ships were intoxicated after a New Year's Eve
party, or whatever), and some of these reasons may again make the
collision appear to have been inevitable from some point of view or
other. But inevitability always depends on point of view, and it is
always possible to find a point of view from which events are not inevitable. Social structure is always changing, and the ability of a political
party to maintain its popularity depends on its ability to find new
sources of support as old ones decline. The American Democratic Party
does not today rest upon the same electoral coalition that Roosevelt
forged during the New Deal era (Nile, Verba, and Petrocik, 1981); the
German CDU is no longer based as largely on Catholic votes as it was in
the 1950s (Feist *et al.*, 1978). The fact that the social basis of Labour
voting remained in 1979 similar to what it had been fifteen years before

means that the decline in the size of that social base led to a decline in the number of people voting Labour. It does not mean that new supporters could not have been found to replace those who had been lost.

Moreover, the decline in Labour voting is not only attributable to changes in social structure. We have already seen that at least as important is the fact that supporters were lost between 1966 and 1970 before the decline in the party's social base began. It seems probable that 1983 also saw loss of votes in greater numbers than the declining social base can account for. Had Labour voting remained as far above the predicted vote in Figure 3.2 at the time of the 1970, 1974, and 1979 elections as it was in 1966, then the decline in the social basis of Labour voting would still have left Labour with more voters than the Tories, all other things being equal.

### Summary and implications

In this chapter we have investigated the way in which the social characteristics of our samples have changed over the twenty-year period of our study. We have seen how some changes have been the result of government policies while others have simply reflected demographic processes, with new voters being typified by somewhat different characteristics than those who died. We also attempted to see what changes in party support might have been anticipated from these changes, all other things being equal. In that context we saw that a decline in the Labour vote would have followed naturally from demographic and other changes.

But our analysis does not point to an inevitable decline in Labour voting. What it does point to is the fact that Labour's decline has at least two distinct aspects which have to be anlysed separately. One of these relates to the changing size of the social groups from which Labour received support in 1964, and the other to the changing proportions supporting Labour within those groups. Since the groups define the class structure that underpinned Labour voting, this latter type of change constitutes a decline in class voting. In the next chapter we will look more closely at the manner in which social structure changed during the period of our concern, so as to evaluate the possibility that the two sources of decline were not independent of each other. At the same time we will discover a variety of contaminating influences that have to be taken into account in any more probing analysis of the nature of the changes that took place.

# 4
# EVALUATING
# THE DECLINE IN
# CLASS VOTING

The purpose of this chapter is to identify the real extent and timing of the decline of class voting, by taking account of other features of contemporary politics with which this decline can easily be confused. In Chapter 3 we considered social class in terms of the individual characteristics that we found to be associated with this concept in Chapter 1. Indeed, we shall have to look even more closely at the effects of these individual characteristics in Chapter 5. However, before we can proceed with that investigation we need to take a step back- wards from the study of particular social characteristics, their changing distribution and their changing effects, to look at social structure as a whole, and the effects on class alignment of any changes that may have occurred in the overall structure of social class. In order to do this, we will have to look beyond the narrow notion of class alignment, as indexed by the correlation between class and voting choice, to two major developments in contemporary British politics identified by Butler and Stokes (1974, p. 206) as strands that are 'consistent with . . . the weakening of the class alignment'. These are the decline in electoral turnout and the rise in minor party voting.

So what we attempt to do in this chapter is to peel back the skin of an onion (as it were) layer by layer to see what is going on beneath. The discussion becomes somewhat technical at times. This is because as each type of change is isolated and identified it has to be held constant, so that other types of change can show themselves. Holding something constant is difficult, and different procedures have had to be adopted in holding constant different types of change. Each of these procedures has to be justified before we can proceed. For those who are willing to take the justifications on trust, these passages can be skimmed or omitted completely. However, the chapter as a whole should not be ignored by those who find it somewhat technical, as its findings are of central importance in the chapters to come. But the important things *are* the findings, *not* the manner in which they are computed.[1]

## Class loyalty and class profile

The class alignment is usually seen as relating to the degree of difference between the proportions in each of two classes voting for the same major party (cf. Butler and Stokes, p. 175). So changes in class alignment can be thought of as being related to changes in these differences between proportions, as illustrated in Figure 4.1. We shall refer to such changes in terms of changing *loyalty* of each class group to

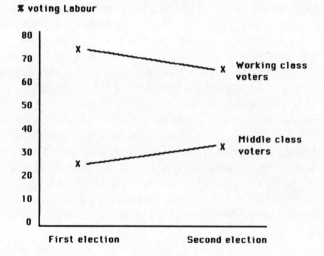

Figure 4.1.   A hypothetical example of reducing separation between two class groups

the party whose support comes mainly from that class. But to view class loyalty as identical with class alignment is only possible so long as each voter can be unambiguously assigned to one of the class groups. If this is to be done then doubtful cases must either be arbitrarily assigned to one class or another or else removed from consideration.

[1] This chapter is largely based on an article entitled 'Demographic and Political Components in the Decline of British Class Voting' published in *Electoral Studies* in 1982. I am grateful to Butterworths, the publishers, for allowing me to make use of material already employed there.

Both of these strategies are overly simplistic,[2] so perhaps a less straight-forward view is to be preferred. In such a view, the class structure might be seen as containing three elements: a working class, a middle class, and an intermediate group of unclassifiable individuals. This group might consist of those who refused to place themselves in a particular class when asked to do so, or those whose occupation does not have a clear class status. If we employ multiple indicators of class status, as we did earlier, then the intermediate group would consist of individuals with mixed class characteristics (having perhaps come from a working-class home but achieved middle-class occupational status).

However the intermediate group is populated, it is clear that its size relative to the two class groups is of fundamental importance in deter-mining the extent of class alignment. The degree of class alignment is limited by the size of this group: if ever a point were reached at which it were found impossible to classify anyone at all as either working class or middle class, then the class alignment would have vanished. On the other hand, as long as this is not the case, the extent of class alignment will also depend on the relative attractions of the two major parties for members of each class.

Of course, even a three group class structure may represent a con-siderable oversimplification of a reality in which individuals tend towards solid or mixed-class characteristics in gradations whose number depends upon the number of characteristics we think it important to consider. And if we have more than three gradations of class, then our focus on the size of the mixed-class group must give way to a focus on the shape of the distribution of class characteristics: what we shall call the class *profile* of the electorate (see Figure 4.5). Moreover there will be additional complications to take into account, in the shape of changes in turnout and minor party voting, to mention just two; but let us dwell a little longer on the implications of a three-group class structure.

The best predictions of voting choice based on class in Britain are obtained when class is viewed as an underlying phenomenon indi-cated by a number of social characteristics (Rose, 1974a, p. 41). Which

---

[2] If doubtful cases are forced into one class or another then the degree of separation between the voting preferences of members of each class will be reduced to the extent of the mistakes that are made. (If the assignment is truly arbitrary, on average one mistake will be made for every two such arbitrary assignments.) If they are excluded, then the degree of separation observed for the remainder will be a misleading indication of the extent of class alignment.

particular characteristics are employed as indicators depends on the view one takes of social processes, but the view one derives from the Butler and Stokes analysis we presented in Chapter 1 is of partisanship being based first of all on inheritance (best indicated by parents' class and parents' party), which for many people defines their initial class status, and then modified by education, occupation, and housing: with union membership, religion, and local environment playing supporting roles (we already saw in Chapter 1 how the last two of these characteristics do not in fact add anything to an explanation encompassing the other six). Butler and Stokes show clearly (p. 101) how individuals with mixed-class characteristics are less likely to vote for any particular political party.

The number of voters with mixed-class characteristics will depend partly on the interactions of a number of demographic trends. Increases in union membership, private housing, educational opportunities, and white-collar occupations all provide the chance for individuals who inherited one variety of partisanship to acquire characteristics associated with another. The quicker the rate of demographic change, the more frequent will be the opportunities for acquiring mixed characteristics. By contrast, a slow-down in the rate of demographic change will necessarily result in due course in a reduction in the size of the group with mixed-class characteristics.

So if the class alignment in Britain is declining, it matters greatly whether it is declining because of lessening loyalty of class members to the party whose support comes mainly from that class, or whether it is declining because of increasing numbers of individuals with mixed-class characteristics. If the former decline is found to be occurring then the problem for the major parties is one of finding ways of increasing their appeal to their traditional class supporters, while if the latter decline is found to be occurring then the decline might be countered by new kinds of appeals to the mixed group. but, more importantly, the decline might reverse itself without the major parties having to take any action at all.

These speculations give rise to a hypothesis which would, if it could be confirmed, be very comforting to the leaders of Britain's Labour Party in 1985. This is that the decline of the class alignment in recent years has been a purely transitory phenomenon brought about by temporary changes in the class structure of the British electorate. Although economic growth was not as rapid in Britain as in many other advanced nations, there was a long period of economic growth during the two decades following the Second World War, which coincided with an increase in the provision of educational opportunities. The effect of these developments will have been to bring into the electorate increasing numbers of children from working-class homes (many of them with Labour-voting parents) who had acquired middle-class characteristics as a result of educational and employment opportunities not available to their parents: new voters with mixed-class characteristics. But in more recent years the pace of economic advance has slackened and educational opportunities have ceased to expand, so that voters entering the electorate since 1970 are less likely to have found themselves with mixed-class characteristics. On this basis we would eventually expect an increase in the class alignment to cancel out the decline of recent years.

Superficial support for this hypothesis can be gleaned from an analysis of the extent of class-based voting in the General Election of 1979, as compared with that which was found ten years before. Employing occupational class as a surrogate for the more complex class reality we have sketched,[3] and ignoring the two elections of 1974 as being non-comparable because of the greater than usual support for minor parties, Figure 4.2 nevertheless suggests that the decline in the class alignment of voting choice had been halted by 1979.

But this analysis is much too superficial to be more than suggestive. In the first place we have employed a surrogate for the more complex class reality. In the second place we have ignored (except in excluding the extreme cases of 1974 and 1983) the complicating effects of turn-out and minor party voting. Most importantly, we have not distinguished in our analysis the two different effects we have been at such pains to identify. The first of these we have called the class *loyalty* to major parties, and the second the class *profile* of the electorate. These are both concepts that have to be carefully distinguished from other influences with which they could easily be confused. We shall see in later sections how class loyalty has to be distinguished from the temporary success that a party may have in increasing its appeal in a particular election, and how the effects of the changing class profile of the electorate have to be distinguished from those of the changing class profile of major party voters.

Although Butler and Stokes do not distinguish between different

---

[3] See for example Franklin and Mughan (1978) for a justification of this customary procedure.

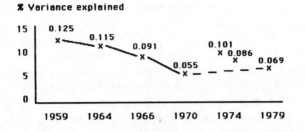

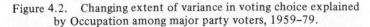

Figure 4.2.    Changing extent of variance in voting choice explained
by Occupation among major party voters, 1959–79.

Coefficients for 1959–70 from Franklin and Mughan (1978, p. 526). Other
coefficients for 1964 to 1970 from these latter data were 0.125, 0.107 and
0.051.

components making up the class alignment in quite the same way
as we do, they do stress the importance of demographic change in
determining the basis of electoral choice. Their analysis of the slowly-
maturing strength of the Labour Party's electoral appeal is essentially
a story of decline in the size of a group with mixed political antecedents
as increasingly more individuals came to be born into households with
a history of Labour voting: a story of the manner in which class
characteristics came slowly to line up with one another for increasing
numbers of individuals, so that there were fewer and fewer in the
mixed class category as the years went by. What we are suggesting as an
initial hypothesis is that the rate of economic growth since the Second
World War, together perhaps with the very success of the Labour Party
in opening up middle-class occupations to working-class penetration,
may have served to reverse this trend, in which case the question of
whether the reversal is temporary or permanent becomes a crucial
question for the future of British politics.

### The data

Before we can investigate the effects of class structure we have to
decide what is to constitute the universe under study. Specifically, are
we interested in the behaviour of major party voters? Or of all voters?
Or of the entire electorate? In the past it has been conventional to
concentrate on major party voters when studying the effects of social
class. We have already implied that such a restrictive approach is

unlikely to be appropriate for studying the 1974 elections where, unless we include minor party voters, we shall almost certainly find an increase in the class voting of that smaller group of voters who did vote for major parties in that year. This consideration impels us towards an analysis of all voters. Moreover, since we are interested in changes in social structure which apply to the entire electorate whether voting or not, we are further impelled towards an analysis of all the respondents to our surveys, including the non-voters. As in past chapters we treat our dependent variable as indexing a preference for Labour, the most class-based party.

Figure 4.3 illustrates the extent to which variance in party choice can be explained by our six social structure variables under different conditions. In this and subsequent analyses in the present chapter, we have insufficient information to be able to include the election of 1983. The two solid lines in the illustration indicate the extent to which the variance in Labour party voting can be explained by these six variables in a multiple regression analysis of major party voters and all voters. The broken line at the top of the illustration shows the extent to which Labour party voting can be explained when the 'best' coding scheme is adopted for each variable in each year, in terms of maximizing the ability of that variable to predict voting choice in that year without

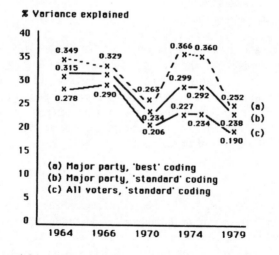

Figure 4.3.   Comparing the results of regression predictions of voting choice under various conditions, 1964–79

regard to comparability. This is included in order to show the extent to which purely predictive capacity has been sacrificed through the adoption of a standard coding scheme for the social structure variables as described in Chapter 3 and the appendix to this book.

Despite quite large differences in the extent to which voting choice is determined by social structure, depending on the universe under study, the two analyses depicted in Figure 4.3 show essentially the same pattern: little change in class voting between 1964 and 1966, then a drop in 1970 followed by an apparently temporary recovery in 1974. Interestingly, this recovery in 1974 does not depend on restricting the analysis to major party voters. Even when minor party voting is allowed to count against the explicable variance, we still see a rise in 1974 followed by a drop in 1979 to more or less the level of a decade before. The pattern appears to be cyclical, and taken at face value might have led us to expect a revival of class voting in 1983. The question we have to answer is whether the apparent cycle hides a more fundamental trend, and, if so, what this trend might be.

Before we can approach an answer to this and other questions arising from our initial hypothesis, we need to design a measure of social class which will permit changes in its structure to show themselves. The measure we have adopted is a simple additive index of our six social structural variables. With each variable coded one if it represents a working class characteristic and zero otherwise, the index ranges from zero to six: a zero score indicating no working-class characteristics for a particular respondent and a score of six indicating no middle-class characteristics.[4] In the analysis that follows we employ this index in two different ways: as a measure of the distribution of class character-istics and as a predictor of voting choice. To measure the distribution of class characteristics we regard the index as defining seven class strata, ranging from solid middle class at one end, through increasing and then reducing extents of class ambiguity, to solid working class at the other end. To determine the extent to which class stratification predicts

---

[4] Where a characteristic was not clearly either working class or middle class, or where it could not be determined, an intermediate value of 0.5 was added to the index so as not to produce a bias in favour of the middle class. The index was rounded up to the nearest whole number, so giving a slight bias in the other direction in practice. The possibility of estimating missing data from regression analysis was rejected on the grounds that the analysis would produce different estimates in different years, and so lose us the comparability between years that is so important for this investigation.

voting choice, we measure the differences of means in Voting Choice, within and between all strata to find the amount of variance in Voting Choice that can be explained by the stratification scheme. As a first stage in this analysis, Figure 4.4 illustrates the extent to which variance in Voting Choice can be explained by the class stratification index for each of the universes under study (voters and respondents), and compares the results with regression results in order to demonstrate the extent to which explanatory power has again been lost, this time through creation of an additive index. The reason why this second simplification is necessary (the first was the use of a standard coding scheme) will become apparent as we proceed. For the present all that is necessary is to note that, in broad outline, the pattern of variance explained in Figure 4.4 follows the same lines as that explained in the two regression analyses presented in Figure 4.3.

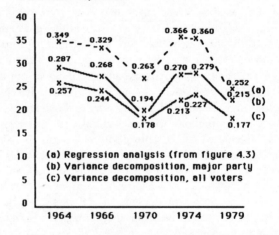

Figure 4.4.    Comparing variance decompositions of voting choice by social strata with regression predictions from the stratification variables, 1964–79

## Changes in class profile

We can discover the proportion of individuals with different mixtures of class characteristics simply by counting the numbers falling into each of the seven class strata defined by our additive index. But the effects of profile on class alignment are by definition only felt among major party voters, while changes in class characteristics apply to the whole electorate. Between the electorate and major party voters there stand two circumstances that vary from election to election quite independently of changes in the profile of the electorate. These are the extent of *turnout* and of *minor party voting*, and they can have two different sorts of effects on the class alignment.

In the first place, as already made evident in Figures 3 and 4, the extent of abstention and minor party voting limits the size of the major party vote. The smaller the major party vote as a proportion of possible votes, the less variance in voting choice can be explained by class loyalty. So changes in the size of the minor party voting group from election to election will affect the class alignment, as will changes in the number of non-voters. At the same time, turnout and minor party voting interact with changing class characteristics of the electorate to affect the class profile of the major party vote. It has often been held that a low turnout benefits the Conservatives, which implies that differences in turnout are not always equally distributed among different class strata. In the same way, there is no reason to suppose that minor party voters will be taken equally from all class strata. Indeed, there is not even any reason to suppose that the class profile of minor party and non-voters will remain the same over time, so that the same extent of turnout and minor party voting will not necessarily have the same effect on the class alignment of major party voters in different elections.[5]

Figure 4.5 illustrates the changing class profile of major party voters, minor party voters, and the whole electorate in a series of five histograms, one for each of our election years.[6] In each histogram the cross-hatched portion represents major party voters, the shaded portion

[5] When dealing with minor party voting we are interested in both the class profile and also the extent of minor party voting. When dealing with turnout, we are concerned with class profile, but extent is much less important. Non-voting does not affect the electoral outcome except in so far as non-voters are drawn disproportionately from different class strata, and this is why we do not include an analysis of the whole electorate in Figures 3 or 4.

[6] Since there was little time available between the two elections of 1974 for changes in social structure to take place, any differences between the class profiles shown by our two samples will have been largely the result of sampling fluctuations, and for demographic purposes the two samples have been taken together. For other purposes they are treated separately. Because of small numbers of respondents falling into the extreme middle-class and working-class strata, the top two and bottom two strata have been taken together in Figure 4.5.

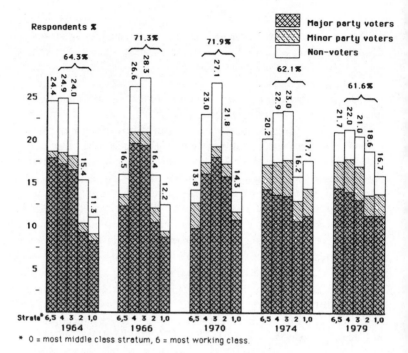

Figure 4.5.   Changing frequency distribution (class profile) of
respondents in different class strata, 1964–79

represents minor party voters, and the unshaded portion represents
non-voters.[7] The whole of each histogram (cross-hatched, shaded, and

[7] It is interesting to note that in none of the years under investigation does
the fraction of the population with coherent characteristics (at least five of the
six characteristics typical of one class) exceed 38 per cent (20.2 + 17.7 in 1974),
and the proportion with totally coherent characteristics (six out of six) is of
course much smaller (only 11 per cent). This tiny fraction of the electorate
contains the two 'ideal type' class groups similar to those employed by Rose
(1974a, p. 509) but smaller because defined on the basis of more characteristics.
Even among the larger fraction containing what we might term the 'near ideal
type' class groups, we shall see that the top and bottom strata in Figure 4.7 show
voting choice to be very strongly determined by class factors. On average, some
86 per cent of major party voters in strata 0, 1,5, and 6 voted for the party of
their class, explaining 57 per cent of variance in voting choice *for these individuals*
in 1964. But the overall effect of this powerful structuring is diluted because the
majority of the population finds itself in ambiguous positions within the class
structure. If we discount those in stratum 3, count one third each for everyone in
strata 2 and 4, and two-thirds each for everyone in strata 1 and 5, in 1964 we find
that an equivalent of only 40 per cent of the sample is able to play a part in

unshaded) thus represents the class profile of the entire electorate during one election year, standardized so that the area under each complete histogram is the same. Because the histograms are standardized they somewhat exaggerate the changes that take place from election year to election year. Some of these changes will have been caused by increases in the size of the electorate which, if they occur unevenly, will cause some strata to appear to shrink. But this exaggeration makes it easier to grasp the nature of the changes in class structure that took place in Britain over the fifteen-year span. What we see is effectively a wave-form travelling across the class spectrum from left to right, whose ultimate effect is, by 1979, to increase somewhat the size of the middle-class strata at the expense of the working- and mixed-class strata, but which in intervening years had the effect of increasing the proportion of the population temporarily finding itself in the mixed-class group. Depending on whether we take stratum 3 as the only mixed stratum, or whether we include the intermediate strata 2 and 4 as well (shown by the bracketed percentages across the top of the chart), we get slightly different pictures of the changing proportion of those with mixed class characteristics, but on either definition the proportion with such characteristics rose dramatically in 1966 (giving rise to the fundamental change in the shape of the distribution in that year) and later began a decline which was still continuing in 1979; and on either definition the proportion had, by 1974, returned to roughly equal that of a decade before.[8]

This is not quite the picture to comfort Britain's Labour party, since it appears that the temporary increase we thought we might find in the proportion of those with mixed-class characteristics was very temporary indeed, and that the class structure had more or less stabilized again by 1974, though with a larger middle-class component. However, the

explaining variance in voting choice. In the same election, therefore, the actual proportion of variance we can explain (0.349, see Figure 4.3) is over 80 per cent of its reasonable maximum. These considerations provide some sort of answer for those who wonder why, if class was supposed to be the basis of British politics, so little variance could be explained in voting choice even in a period when class structuring was thought to be extensive.

[8] This rapid transformation of the distribution of class characteristics is hard to explain substantively, and may indeed be an artifact of the particular samples we are employing (see Chapter 3). However, these data are the only ones we now have available to investigate the events of the past twenty years, and any contamination they may contain must be analysed and corrected for, whether it is a contamination that reflects real events in the world that was sampled, or merely a poor sample.

effect of changing class profiles on variance explained is hard to compute by eye, affected as it is by differential turnout and minor party
voting. Table 4.1, whose import is summarized in Figure 4.6, peels

Table 4.1.   *Demographic influences on class voting removed,*
*1964–1979\**

| Influence | 1964–66 | 1966–70 | 1970–74 | Feb–Oct | 1974–79 |
|---|---|---|---|---|---|
| Total change in variance explained from election to election, uncorrected | –0.019 | –0.074 | 0.076 | 0.009 | –0.064 |
| Correction for electorate profile | 0.039 | –0.007 | –0.038 | 0.000 | 0.003 |
| Correction for minor party vote profile | 0.001 | –0.006 | –0.028 | 0.000 | 0.004 |
| Correction for turnout profile | –0.002 | 0.001 | 0.000 | 0.000 | 0.006 |
|  | 0.019 | –0.086 | 0.010 | 0.009 | –0.051 |
| Extent of minor party voting | 0.006 | 0.008 | –0.041 | 0.005 | 0.014 |
|  | 0.025 | –0.078 | –0.031 | 0.014 | –0.037 |

\* We make no corrections for class profiles between the two sections of 1974.
  See footnote 6.

away these complicating factors by holding constant first the class
profile of the entire electorate, then additionally the class profiles of
minor party and non-voters. Finally, the table (and the illustration)
take into account the changing size of the minor party voting group.[9]
The lowest line in the illustration thus represents the changing extent of
class voting, net of those contaminating influences which arise from
demographic change. The corrections shown in Table 1 derive from
holding the circumstances (the number of people in each class group)

[9] The effects of the changing size of each group on variance explained is
already known from Figure 4.4, where it is represented by the extent of convergence or divergence of the lines standing for each universe. The effects of the
changing class profile of each universe on variance explained can be estimated by
holding it constant: giving more weight to strata whose numbers had declined and
less to strata whose numbers had increased.

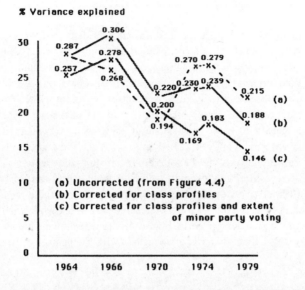

Figure 4.6. Comparing variance decompositions of voting choice by social strata, corrected for changes in class profile, with uncorrected results, 1964–79

constant and comparing the variance explained when no change in class profile is permitted with the variance actually explained in each year.[10]

These corrections have the effect of changing the general pattern observed in Figure 4.4 (and summarized by the broken line at the top of Figure 4.6) of a cyclical movement in class voting with no discernible trend, to one of a cyclical movement with a clear downward trend, a large part of the apparent resurgence in class voting in the two elections of 1974 having been caused in fact by changes in the class profile of the electorate and by changes in minor party voting (see Table 4.1).

[10] To take an example, the variance explained by social structure decline by 0.019 between 1964 and 1966 (the first entry in Table 4.1 is equivalent to the difference between 0.287 and 0.268 on the broken line in Figure 4.6). But the correction for electorate profile of +0.039 shown on the next row of the table indicates that had the class structure of the electorate remained constant between those two years, the actual change in variance explained would have been an *increase* of 0.020 (0.039–0 019). In actual fact, the correction was arrived at by first observing the variance explained in 1966 in a simulated data set which had the same number of respondents in each class stratum as observed in 1964 but the mean support for the Labour Party observed in 1966, and comparing this coefficient (0.206) with the uncorrected coefficient (0.268). 0.306–0.268 would equal 0.039 but for rounding errors.

## Changes in class loyalty

The downward trend in explained variance evident in Figure 4.6 can also be uncovered through a complementary approach to that which we have so far employed. If we focus on class loyalty to major parties, rather than upon variance explained, then the changing sizes of these class groups becomes irrelevant to the picture we uncover. What we look at are changes in the degree of separation of the class strata in terms of their propensity to vote for the Labour party, as previewed at the start of this chapter, in Figure 4.1. In Figure 4.7 the solid traces reflect the actual percentages voting Labour among major party voters and the broken traces represent estimates derived from regression analysis of the trend lines that best fit these solid traces. Clearly these trend lines are tending to converge, in much the same way as shown in the simplified example that was given in Figure 4.1 above, showing that loyalty to the party of their class was growing less with the passage of time.

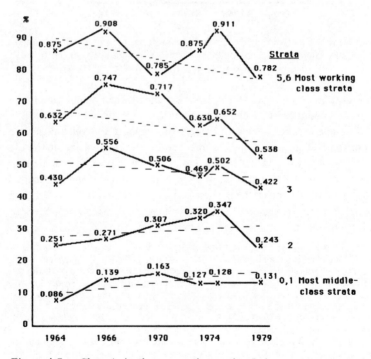

Figure 4.7.    Changes in the proportion voting Labour among voters in different class strata with best-fitting trends (broken lines), 1964–7a

Figure 4.8 summarizes the message of Figure 4.7 by averaging the working-class and middle-class groups.[11] The illustration shows a swing to the Conservatives in both class groups between 1970 and 1974 which did not in fact occur (though it is also evident in Figure 4.7) and which indicates that the true swing in the other direction was entirely the effect of increasing numbers of individuals falling into Labour-voting strata. Such increases are shown in Figure 4.5 to have been extensive between the two years in question.

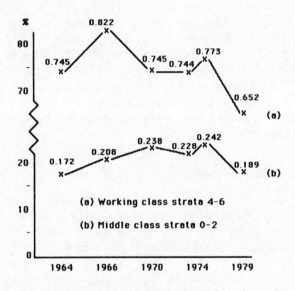

Figure 4.8. Changes in percentage voting Labour in working and middle class strata, 1964–79

So Figure 4.8 shows unsurprisingly that support for the Labour party among voters in working-class strata moved in step with swings in the electoral fortunes of that party nationally. When the Labour party gained votes, the working classes showed more class loyalty, and when the Labour party lost votes these strata showed less class loyalty. Bearing in mind that working-class strata comprise more people than middle-class strata (see Figure 4.5), it is clear that changes in class voting in the working-class strata will have had a greater effect than

[11] The weights accorded to the different strata during this averaging were derived by treating all six surveys as a single sample, and taking the average size of each stratum from this pooled data.

countervailing changes in the middle class. Over the years of our study, class voting in general will have tended to move in step with the electoral fortunes of the Labour Party.

Figure 4.8 also simplifies the diversity of swings evident in Figure 4.7 and shows, on average, the middle- and working-class strata moving in parallel except between 1966 and 1970 when the two groups converged considerably. But the illustration also shows the middle-class swings to have been generally less than the working-class swings. So while we generally see opposite effects on class loyalty to each party in the middle and working classes (middle-class loyalty goes down when working-class loyalty goes up, and vice versa, except in 1970), these effects are by no means equal; and the effect of working-class swings on variance explained will thus dominate not only because of the larger number of individuals involved in these swings, but also because of their greater amplitude. Some means will have to be found to correct for this phenomenon before the true underlying trend in class loyalty to major parties can be discovered.

### Swings in electoral fortunes

In a country in which the working class is larger than the middle class, it is only to be expected that swings in electoral fortunes will influence the apparent degree of class loyalty to major parties (as well as the other way around). To win elections the Conservative Party must have support from working-class individuals, and a swing to the Conservatives which brings more working-class support will reduce the incidence of class voting while a swing in the other direction will increase the incidence of class voting.

To estimate the underlying trend in the decline of class loyalty we need to be able to estimate the effects on variance explained of temporary swings in electoral fortunes. Unfortunately, this cannot be done with the same lack of ambiguity as with demographic changes. Much depends on the extent to which different class strata are assumed to be affected by the swings. We have shown that working-class strata are more susceptible to these effects than middle-class strata. However, to decide precisely what proportion of the effect of swing belongs with each class stratum is clearly beyond the bounds of reasonable possibility, since changes in class loyalty may be causes as well as consequences of swing. What we can do is to try out a number of different ways of apportioning the swing component, in order to establish a range of possibilities within which the correct result probably lies; and to map out the effects of these different assumptions on the residual decline in class loyalty. To this end we consider the class spectrum in three groups, two comprising strata 0 to 2 and 4 to 6, and a mixed group comprising stratum 3. The range of possible weights given to the susceptibilities of each group to the effects of swing are set by the following three rules:

(1) There should be as little movement as possible in the mixed-class stratum since, if class loyalty is all there is left to change between elections, this can hardly be expected to affect those with totally mixed-class characteristics;

(2) No class stratum should shift the balance of its party allegiance consistently in the same direction from election to election as the general pattern, since in this case we have given insufficient weight to the effects of swing on that stratum; and

(3) No class stratum should shift the balance of its party allegiance consistently in the opposite direction from election to election as the general pattern, since in this case we have given too much weight to the effects of swing on that stratum.

These rules did not yield a unique set of weights whose ascription to each class stratum would serve to cancel out the effects of swings in electoral fortunes. However, they did lead to the establishment of boundary conditions: initial and final weights which, when applied to different class strata, had the effect of cancelling to a greater or lesser extent the spurious influence of swing on apparent class alignment.[12]

Figure 4.9 illustrates the consequences of these various assumptions by plotting the degree of separation of the two class groups under the initial and final weighting assumptions for swing (solid lines). The broken lines in the illustration show the boundaries of the values that could be taken by these plots under the most drastic conditions, where susceptibility to swing altered for each stratum from election to

---

[12] The weight that had to be ascribed to the mixed-class stratum in order to meet rule (1) was quickly found to be 1.25. Rule (2) turned out to give a lower limit of unity to the proportion of weight that could be ascribed to the working-class strata, while rule (3) gave an upper limit of 0.7 to the proportion of weight that could be ascribed to the middle-class strata. So starting from an initial position which ascribed susceptibility to swing in each group in the ratios 0.7 (middle class): 1.25 (mixed stratum): 1 (working class), the weights accorded to middle-class strata were progressively reduced in steps of 0.2 down to a minimum of 0.3, while the weight accorded to the working-class strata was progressively increased in the same increments up to a maximum of 1.4.

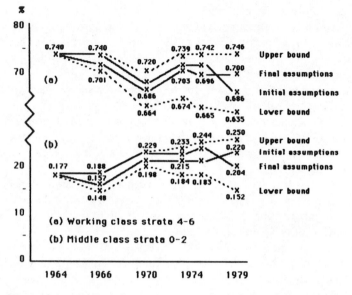

Figure 4.9.   Projected proportions voting Labour among working
class and middle class strata when swing is held constant under
various assumptions, 1964–79

election in such a way as either consistently to maximize an upward
trend or maximize a downward trend in the resulting estimate of class
loyalty.

The illustration has to be interpreted with care. Although variations
in class loyalty could cause the loyalty of one class to take any route
within the broken lines bounding the possibilities for that class, the
choice of route for one class also determines the choice of route for the
other, since less weight given to middle-class strata necessarily requires
a compensating additional weight to be given to working-class strata.
At the limit, if the working-class projections follow the upper boundary
illustrated for the working class then the middle-class projections must
follow the upper boundary shown for the middle class, and vice versa
for the other limiting case. In fact, any route chosen for one class will
result in a roughly parallel route for the opposite class, with the
proviso that the degree of separation of the two classes is always
reduced between 1966 and 1970 by a minimum of 6.7 per cent, while
the degree of separation may be further reduced between 1974 and
1979, but only by a maximum of 3.6 per cent.

Indeed, the initial solution illustrated by the (generally outer) pair of solid lines in Figure 4.9 turns out to show the maximum degree of convergence between the voting choice of different classes occurring during both these periods (9.1 and 3.6 per cent); while other solutions show less convergence in both periods. The initial solution is the most aesthetically satisfying, as it shows reductions in class voting within one class being mirrored by reductions in the other class, and it is also the most parsimonious solution in that it produces the minimum correction for the effect of swing consistent with the three rules listed above. However, neither of these considerations need necessarily lead to the truth, and in what follows we shall average the effect of the first and final corrections, bearing in mind that the differences between the two are not great (see Table 4.2).

Despite the range of possibilities, our findings are quite clear. Figure 4.9 shows a reduction in loyalty by each class occurring between 1966 and 1970 that was very like the imaginary reduction illustrated in the hypothetical Figure 4.1 above, and which was much greater than any reduction occurring before or since. The illustration is effectively a corrected version of Figure 4.8, and the same corrections can be applied to the calculations shown in Table 4.1 to derive the residual extent of class loyalty in the two universes (voters and respondents) that we have been considering. Table 4.2 lists these corrections in terms of both average and boundary values, and applies them to both universes after correction has already been made for demographic influences contained in Table 4.1. The range of possibilities deriving from the boundary values is only large between 1974 and 1979 (±0.013). It is moderate between 1964 and 1966 (±0.009) and small at other times (no more than ±0.006).

Figure 4.10 summarizes these findings for both universes, with the broken line at the top of the illustration showing the changes in variance explained for major party voters uncorrected for swing (taken from Figure 4.6) and the broken lines at the foot of the illustration showing the same changes as the lowest solid line, but each adopting one of the extreme weighting strategies in correcting for swing. The lowest lines in Figure 4.10 show clearly that the consequence of correcting for swing is again to alter the view we must take of the changing pattern of class loyalty, which we first thought to be cyclical (Figure 4.4), then cyclical on a downward trend (Figure 4.6), to one that is not cyclical at all (Figure 4.10), but rather consists in a sudden drop in class loyalty occurring mainly between 1966 and 1970, with much less change thereafter.

Table 4.2. Effects of swing on class voting removed, 1964-1979

| Influence | 1964-66 | 1966-70 | 1970-74 | Feb-Oct | 1974-79 |
|---|---|---|---|---|---|
| Change in variance explained from election to election corrected for class profiles (Table 4.1) | +0.019 | -0.086 | +0.010 | +0.009 | -0.051 |
| Correction for swing | -0.041 ± 009 <br> -0.023 ± 009 | +0.018 ± 006 <br> -0.069 ± 006 | +0.008 ± 003 <br> +0.018 ± 003 | -0.011 ± 004 <br> -0.002 ± 004 | +0.033 ± 013 <br> -0.019 ± 013 |
| Extent of minor party voting | +0.006 <br> -0.017 ± 009 | +0.008 <br> -0.061 ± 006 | -0.041 <br> -0.023 ± 003 | +0.005 <br> +0.003 ± 004 | +0.014 <br> -0.005 ± 013 |

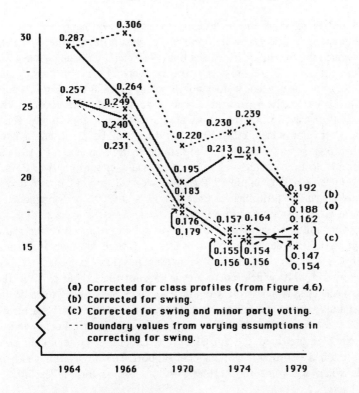

Figure 4.10. Comparing the results of variance decompositions when swing is held constant with those obtained when only class profiles were held constant for major party and all voters, 1964–79

## Summary and implications

Although we have been able to distinguish a number of different components which together determine the degree of class alignment, only one of these shows any systematic change over the period between 1964 and 1979. This is the extent of class loyalty to major parties which declined precipitously during a very short period. Other components, and particularly those associated with demographic change in the class-composition of the electorate, have been subject to cyclical effects which have largely worked themselves out over the period we have been examining. So our initial hypothesis, which posited a transitory decline in class alignment because of temporary changes in the class profile of the electorate, could not be confirmed.

But in rejecting the preliminary hypothesis we uncovered a set of interacting influences which appear to constitute a rather complex mechanism. In particular, class voting is affected by a swing in electoral fortunes such that class voting goes up when the Labour party does well, and down when it does poorly. Thus in 1983 the very fact that the Labour party performed so badly would lead us to expect a low extent of class voting, though we are not yet in a position to say which is cause and which effect (this question will be discussed in later chapters). In so far as the partial data currently available for this most recent election permits estimates to be made, class voting was in fact no lower in 1983 than in 1979 (indeed we shall see in Chapter 6 that it was actually a little higher) once Labour's absolute performance had been taken into account by adjusting for the effects of swing.

Our ability to pin-point both the nature and occasion of the mainspring in the decline of class voting in Britain has two important implications. In the first place, something must have happened between 1966 and 1970 which led to a swing against the Labour party in the working-class strata at the same time as there was a swing towards the Labour party in the middle-class strata, as we saw so clearly in Figure 4.8. So we are able to look for events occurring within a short period of time that increased the appeal of the Labour party to middle-class voters while costing it working-class support. This observation will help us when we come to consider possible reasons for the decline, in Chapter 7.

In the second place, we have managed to uncover several contaminating influences that affect the extent of class voting as measured by conventional means. Because all the variables that concern us are interrelated, each one of them is affected by extraneous influences on all of them. Taken one at a time, each acts in part as an indicator for the others, so that a decline in the importance of all class variables will, other things being equal, be reflected in a decline in any one of them. These sorts of considerations will go some way towards explaining the volatility in partial regression effects that was noticed in Chapter 3. The contaminating influences may have implications that go beyond the problems of measurement that they most immediately entail; but from the viewpoint of our present concerns, the most important implication is that the contaminating influences will themselves have to be taken into account in the more probing analysis of changing effects of social class that we are going to undertake in the next chapter.

# 5

# THE POTENTIAL FOR RADICAL CHANGE

In this chapter we will consider the nature of the decline in class voting in more detail than we have done so far. The object is to show how this decline opened the door to explosions in minor party voting such as were seen in 1974 and 1983.[1] Indeed, the decline has gone so far that the potential exists for a major change in the party system.

Whether or not it is realized in any particular election, the existence of a potential for radical change itself constitutes a change in the nature of British politics. Politicians in general and those representing new parties in particular can reasonably aspire to more than just altering the party balance from one Parliament to the next. They can aspire to actually destroying a party of long standing, and replacing it with a new one. The social structures that used to limit the extent of volatility from one election to the next also made the existing party system sacrosanct. The present chapter seeks to prove that this is no longer so, and that the continued presence of Labour and Conservative as major parties in 1983 may be regarded as little more than accidental.

Here we explore the decline of class voting in terms of changes in the importance of individual variables associated with the concept of social class. To this end we begin by defining a causal model which depicts the linkages that existed in 1964 between the particular variables concerned. This model, which is the one that was previewed in Chapter 1, will clarify the way in which some features of class voting depended on others for their effects. In particular it will enable us to show that, when class voting was at its height in 1964, two variables (Parents' Class and Respondent's Occupation) had to be considered *central* to any traditional conception of class-based voting choice. Other social structural variables performed a supportive role. Reassessing this model in subsequent years permits us to establish the manner in which the decline of class voting took place over the following decade, and show

[1] This chapter restates the main findings of an article entitled 'How the Decline of Class Voting Opened the Way to Radical Change in British Politics' which was published in the *British Journal of Political Science* in 1984. I am grateful to Cambridge University Press for permitting me to use this material.

how the variables most central to the concept of class voting in 1964 are those whose importance in structuring voting choice decline the most. It will be suggested that these are also the variables that previously did most to inoculate the electorate against radical change. So the modest decline in class voting that was apparent in Chapter 4 when class was measured in terms of an additive index will be seen to mask a more dramatic decline in the ability of these central variables to structure partisanship. It is this that has left us with a party system ripe for extensive changes.

At the same time the analysis will shed light on a second strand in recent voting studies: the observed paradox that although class has become a poorer predictor of voting choice at the individual level, it has at the same time increased its dominance in a constituency-level analysis of characteristics and electoral results. This finding suggests that the class characteristics of 'people around here' may have become more important electorally than the class characteristics of 'people like me', giving rise to an apparent area effect of class to replace the individual effect that used to be prevalent (Miller, 1978). Our own analysis can contribute to an understanding of this paradox because even while most class variables have declined as predictors of individual voting choice, some have actually seen their effects enhanced; and the particular variables whose effects have increased are those which might well be related to processes of group opinion formation likely to be involved in an area effect.

In this way we will establish that the social forces which sustained the British two-party system in 1974 no longer constituted a class system as this had previously been understood. In particular, the social mechanisms which remained in 1974 for transmitting party choice from generation to generation, and for reinforcing and sustaining this choice through adult life, were no longer such as to support any particular party system. The parties which dominated British politics in 1974 did so because they were established, *not* because they were class-based. Any other parties could have benefited equally from the support in question, and in Scotland it seems that the support for Scottish Nationalism in that year was a case in point. The same support could sustain a system that lacked one or both of today's major parties, or which incorporated additional parties, no less readily (and probably no less shakily) than it now sustains the traditional system of voting choice.

## The model

The seven variables we are investigating (six representing social influences, together with voting choice) can be arranged in temporal sequence so as to constitute the model of voting choice that was already introduced in Chapter 1. There we saw that the seven variables we have been concerned with can be spread out on a five-point temporal scale, with Parents' Party and Respondent's Education occupying joint second place between Parents' Class and Respondents Occupation, and with Respondent's Home Tenure and Union Membership similarly tying for fourth place between Occupation and Vote. Figure 5.1 illustrates this model in a preliminary fashion, showing the more important uncontrolled correlations between these variables in 1964.[2]

Some of the coefficients in Figure 5.1 will of course be spurious consequences of prior effects, while others will be the work (in large or small part) of intervening variables.[3] But the major point to emerge is the relatively small magnitude of many of the coefficients shown there, and particularly of some of those between social influences. Social structure in Britain is not particularly coherent, and the possession of one attribute typical of some class does not bring with it a very high probability for possession of any other particular attribute typical of that class. It is for this reason that the powerful structuring of voting choice that we saw in Figure 1.2 is diluted in its impact on the

[2] The coefficients are Pearsonian product-moment correlations. The model differs from the only other British voting model of similar (or greater) complexity in a number of respects. See Himmelweit *et al.* (1981), especially pp. 68–71. As pointed out in Chapter 2, Himmelweit and associates were concerned with individuals all of whom entered the electorate together, and each of whom thus had the opportunity of voting in an identical number of General Elections. Past voting behaviour becomes a plausible component of such a model, replacing the role of parents' party in our own model and dominating the resulting picture at the expense of such variables as housing and union membership. Moreover, attitudinal variables are introduced as mediating between social characteristics and voting choice. However, the major difference between this model and my own is the inclusion of a variable, educational attainment, which I eliminated because, despite its large effect for the small number of individuals who did receive higher education, it added very little to the overall variance explained.

[3] Spurious relationships arise when the two variables involved are both consequential upon the same prior influence (Parents' Party and Respondent's Occupation are both the consequence of Parents' Class, and do turn out to be only spuriously related when this is taken into account – see Figure 5.3). Intervening variables (such as Parents' Party) may be required to transmit effects between more distant variables (such as Parents' Class and Respondent's Union Membership).

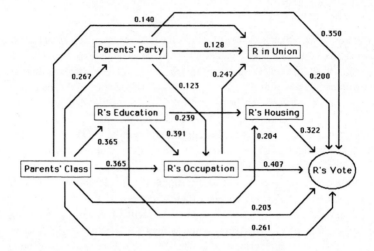

Figure 5.1.    A preliminary model of class voting, showing selected correlations between variables for all respondents in 1964*

* Because of missing data, the N varies from 1,208 to 1,773

electorate as a whole: very few people have all the attributes associated with either the working or middle class (only 7 per cent in 1964).[4]

In order to refine the model presented in Figure 5.1, it is necessary to eliminate the links that are wholly spurious (or wholly the work of intervening variables) and adjust the weight given to other links to reflect the fact that some of them will be partly spurious (or partly the work of intervening variables). To do this a series of multiple regression analyses can be performed, in which each variable other than parents' class is treated in turn as dependent upon those variables prior in causal sequence. Thus voting choice is initially treated as dependent on all other variables, home tenure as dependent on all but voting choice and union membership, and so on. In each of these analyses the independent variables are eliminated from the equation in turn, to see how much explanatory power they add to the prediction when all other variables have explained as much as they can. If a variable eliminated in this fashion is found to have contributed less than half a per cent to the explained variance it is removed from consideration, and the process repeated for the remaining variables.[5] A large number of

---

[4]    50 plus 38 out of 1,208 (Figure 1.2).
[5]    This is similar to the 'backward elimination' procedure detailed in Draper and Smith (1966, pp. 167–8).

potential links can be eliminated by these means, but there is a complicating factor that has to be borne in mind. This arises from the fact that we not only want to see a model appropriate to a single election, but one in which changes in the importance of particular variables can be traced over a considerable time-span. Since the elimination of any link changes (albeit slightly) the linkages for all other variables, comparisons are only possible between models containing the same links. Thus a linkage found to be important at one election must be included in the model for another election with which comparisons are to be made, even though its importance at that time was slight.

In this fashion, models were established for each pair of successive elections between 1964 and 1979, as well as for certain pairs more widely separated in time. The models including the 1966 and 1970 elections turned out to be severely affected by swings in the electoral fortunes of major parties and also by temporary demographic effects, as anticipated in Chapter 4. However, this same research tells us that demographic effects had worked themselves out by 1974, and we know that the parties were in rough electoral balance both in 1964 and 1974, so that these two elections are comparable in at least two respects.[6] Since the major changes in class voting took place during the intervening decade, as we saw in Chapter 4, we can best gauge the nature of the changes by concentrating on the two elections at which the contaminating influence of other factors will have been least in evidence. So it is upon the model of class voting for 1964 and 1974 that we now focus our attention.

Figure 5.2 differs from Figure 5.1 in showing fewer links between the variables, a number having been found to be either spurious or the work of intervening variables by means of the analysis described above. This time the coefficients illustrated are not correlations but ordinary (unstandardized) partial regression coefficients (see Chapter 1). Moreover, each link is now accompanied by a pair of coefficients: those above each line relate to all respondents in 1964 while those below each line relate to all respondents in 1974. So the coefficient of 0.261 linking Parents' Party to Respondent's Vote for 1964 can be interpreted as the proportion of respondents who would have been expected to vote differently in that year had their parents evinced a

[6] They are non comparable in the extent of minor party voting, but this difficulty will be allowed for in the analysis that follows. All the models were subjected to a number of tests to determine their adequacy, as recommended by Asher (1976, pp. 33–4).

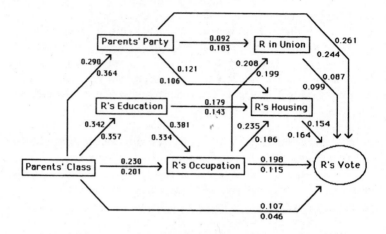

Figure 5.2.    A more refined model of class voting, showing effects (partial unstandardized regression estimates) for all respondents in 1964 (upper coefficients) and 1974 (lower coefficients).*

* Because of missing data, the N varies from 1,208 to 1,773 in 1964 and from 1,106 to 2,453 in 1974.

different party preference, while all other influences remained the same.[7] As in Chapter 1, in speaking of any one respondent these proportions can be turned into probabilities simply by multiplying by 100 and viewing the results as chances out of a hundred. And again, the effects into any node of the model can be summed, so that, for example, the chances of a working-class occupation on the part of a respondent with minimum educational attainments and working-class parents was 61.1 per cent greater in 1964 than were the chances of

[7] The mechanics of causal modelling were described in Chapter 1. All the analyses reported in this paper were performed using 'pairwise' deletion of missing data. The danger inherent in this method lies in the possibility that the case base for some coefficients could be very different from the case base for other co-efficients. In order to guard against the possibility of being misled in this fashion, all the analyses were repeated with missing data being replaced by least-squares estimates of their true values. Happily the results of all these analyses corresponded closely to the results presented here, though the coefficients were generally of a somewhat lower magnitude, reflecting errors in estimation. The data manipulation involved in all these analyses was extensive and could hardly have been attempted without instantaneous access to intermediate findings as different coding schemes were tried and different regression models evaluated. The computer package used was SCSS (Nie, Hull, and Franklin, 1980).

a working-class occupation on the part of one who had neither of these characteristics.

## The extent of class voting in 1964

Is this model one of class voting? It is clear that in 1964 it was reasonable to identify it as such. By 1974, however, no such identification could any longer be made. This is because of changes in two variables included in the model which must have a central part to play in any social mechanism underlying class-based voting behaviour. Occupation is one of these variables, given primacy in almost every study of the electoral impact of British social conditions.[8] The other is Parents' Class. This variable has not always been stressed in British voting studies, because questions about childhood class environment have not always been included in British electoral surveys. However, it is clear that many individuals have a class self-image that does not accord with their occupational status because they view their childhood roots as working class.[9]

More importantly, perhaps, it is clear from Figure 5.2 that the model could never have been one of class voting unless primacy *was* given to parents' class. This is because parents' party preference, already identified as the most powerful determinant of voting choice, need have no class connotation unless it is linked to parents' class in the manner depicted in the model. Without such links it could transmit any variety of partisanship from generation to generation, rather than reinforcing the transmission of class-based preferences in the context of a class-based political system.

So while the model may not in fact be correct (and we cannot prove

---

[8] See for example Butler and Stokes (1974, pp. 70–3); Rose (1974a, pp. 143–52); Crewe, Sarlvik, and Alt (1977, pp. 168–81). The major dissenting voice among researchers into British voting behaviour comes from Patrick Dunleavy who suggests that British voting behaviour is determined not by the social influences people experience in the home, school, and workplace but by real economic interests which have in recent years come to be determined by consumption patterns (see Chapter 2). Because of his focus on interests rather than influences, Dunleavy's analysis falls outside the tradition within which the present argument is constructed.

[9] In all our surveys, respondents were asked to place themselves as working class or middle class. Analysis of responses to this question in the Butler and Stokes 1964 survey shows that two thirds (68.1 per cent) of the individuals whose class self-image conflicted with their occupational status had class origins consistent with this self-image.

it to be correct) it is surely the model that underlay the concept of class-based voting behaviour in Britain.[10] If class really was the basis of British politics, as was generally supposed at least until the mid-1970s, this can only have been true in the context of a model of class voting such as that in Figure 5.2. For features as important as parents' party and home ownership not to constitute exceptions it would have been essential that they be considered consequential upon social class in one manifestation or another.[11]

Indeed, if these two particular variables are to be subsumed within a class-based view of electoral choice, then two manifestations of social class are needed in order to provide the necessary anchorages. The only possible candidates are occupation and parents' class. In what follows these will be referred to as 'central' variables in the model of British class voting. Other variables will be termed 'supportive'.

Viewed from the mid-1980s, when the Labour and Conservative parties are clearly distinguished on a number of salient policy dimensions, it is sometimes hard to remember that many of these policy differences were far more muted twenty years ago. We will see in the next chapter that issue-based preferences played almost no part in party choice in 1964. It is hard to credit the fact, but Butler and King showed that unions (to take an example of a contemporary issue of high salience that divides the major parties) *were not mentioned* in any of the 1964 election addresses given by candidates in their 25 per cent sample (Butler and King, 1964, p. 143); and Conservatives apparently suffered somewhat in the same election because their promise to follow much the same housing policies as Labour was less credible (p. 139). So the power of housing and union membership to predict 1964 partisanship must be attributed to something other than policy differences.

---

[10] The model leaves out certain variables that Butler and Stokes emphasize in their discussion of voting choice, particularly the effects of the local political environment. As pointed out in Chapter 1, these other factors are already subsumed within a model as detailed as the one presented here. A respondent with all six working-class characteristics included in the model is most likely also to live in a heavily working-class environment, and the reverse is true of one with six middle-class characteristics.

[11] Not all researchers would have subsumed the consequences of class within the concept. Rose, for example, (1974b and elsewhere) considers class to be a matter of reinforcing or cross-cutting social characteristics which yield a few 'ideal type' class members with all the characteristics typical of that class. Other members of the population approximate more or less to the ideal. However, Rose does not construct a causal model of class voting, and it is not implausible to suggest that our model underlies even Rose's eclectic approach.

It must be due to the face-to-face contacts among politically homo-geneous groups of people brought about by these social characteristics.

The manner in which the central variables used to anchor the sup-portive variables within a class-based party system is readily seen if we start by reassessing the unique contribution of parents' party preference within the structure depicted in Figure 5.2, along lines introduced in Chapter 1. What the model asserts is that, in 1964, 29 per cent of the effects of Parents' Party were in reality ascribable to the influence of Parents' Class. So of the direct effects of Parents' Party, 7.6 per cent ($= 0.290 \times 0.261$) must be reassigned to the variable prior in causal sequence, as described in Chapter 1.

In this manner, Table 5.1 accumulates the total effects attributable to each variable from direct and indirect influences and then, for variables subsequent to Parents' Class, removes the effects that have been attributed back to variables earlier in causal sequence. The net effect column thus cumulates the additional influence ascribable to each variable after indirect effects have been attributed back as early as possible in causal sequence, and indicates that in 1964 central class variables accounted for 0.387 out of 0.806 (or 48 per cent) of total influences when these were reassigned in a manner consistent with the causal structure of the model.[12]

But even this is not the end of the story. The total effects of occu-pation are reached in Table 5.1 after subtracting influences thought properly to belong to education. But where our objective is to evaluate the impact of central class variables we must bear in mind that most of the influences of Education would not have been felt but for the presence of Occupation to channel them forward to Voting Choice. In other words, the model asserts that education is only influential in so far as it serves to place people in an occupational context which itself has consequences for voting choice. So it can be argued that the net effects of occupation should not be reduced in the same manner as the net effects of other variables. A true assessment of the contribution of central variables to the model in Figure 5.2 requires not only that they be credited with influences they exert indirectly, but also with influences that would not have been exerted by prior variables without

---

[12] It must be emphasized that the attribution of influences to prior variables in this fashion results directly from the causal ordering of the model, which was determined on the basis of theoretical considerations. Once this ordering is established, indirect effects result from the rules of algebra, and do nothing to confirm the correct definition of the model.

Table 5.1. *Direct and indirect effects of central class and other variables calculated from Figure 5.4 for 1964*

| Row no | Effects of | Via | Gross effect | Includes effect | at rows | Net effect |
|---|---|---|---|---|---|---|
| 1 | Parents' Class | Direct | 0.107 | | | 0.107 |
| 2 | | Parents' Party | 0.076 | | | 0.076 |
| 3 | | and Union | 0.002 | | | 0.002 |
| 4 | | and Housing | 0.005 | | | 0.005 |
| | | Education | | | | |
| 5 | | and Housing | 0.009 | | | 0.009 |
| 6 | | and Occupation | 0.026 | | | 0.026† |
| 7 | | and Union | 0.002 | | | 0.002 |
| 8 | | and Housing | 0.005 | | | 0.005 |
| 9 | | Occupation | 0.046 | | | 0.046† |
| 10 | | and Union | 0.006 | | | 0.006 |
| 11 | | and Housing | 0.008 | | | 0.008 |
| | | (Total indirect) | | | | (0.184) |
| | | Total effects | 0.291 | | | 0.291 |
| 13 | Parents' Party | Direct | 0.261 | 0.076 | 2 | 0.185 |
| 14 | | Union | 0.008 | 0.002 | 3 | 0.006 |
| 15 | | Housing | 0.019 | 0.005 | 4 | 0.014 |
| | | (Total indirect) | | | | (0.020) |
| | | Total effects | 0.288 | | | 0.205 |

| | | | | | | |
|---|---|---|---|---|---|---|
| 16 | Education | Housing | 0.028 | 0.009 | 5 | 0.019 |
| 17 | | Occupation | 0.075 | 0.026 | 6 | 0.049* |
| 18 | | and Union | 0.007 | 0.002 | 7 | 0.005* |
| 19 | | and Housing | 0.014 | 0.005 | 8 | 0.009* |
| | | (Total indirect) | | | | (0.082) |
| | | Total effects | 0.124 | | | 0.082 |
| 20 | Occupation | Direct | 0.198 | 0.121 | 6,7,17 | 0.077 |
| 21 | | Union | 0.018 | 0.013 | 7,10,18 | 0.005 |
| 22 | | Housing | 0.036 | 0.022 | 8,11,19 | 0.014 |
| | | (Total indirect) | | | | (0.019) |
| | | Total effects | 0.252 | | | 0.096 |
| 23 | Union | Direct | 0.087 | 0.026 | 3,7,10, 14,18,21 | 0.061 |
| 24 | Housing | Direct | 0.154 | 0.083 | 4,5,8,11, 15,16,19, 22 | 0.071 |
| | *All variables* | Total direct effects | 0.806 | | | 0.501 |
| | | Total indirect effects | | | | (0.305) |
| | | | | | | 0.806 |
| | *central class variables* | Total direct effects | 0.305 | | | 0.184 |
| | | Total indirect effects | | | | 0.203 |
| | | | | | | 0.387 |

† Effects routed via occupation are properly regarded as direct effects of central class variables viewed as a whole (see text).

* Effects routed via occupation total 0.063 to be added to the effects of central class variables in any complete assessment of the role played by central class variables (see text).

their intervention. A suitable adjustment to Table 5.1 to take account of this consideration would add 0.063 to the effects of occupation, bringing the influence of central class variables up to almost 56 per cent of total influences, as shown in Table 5.2.[13]

Table 5.2.    *Components of change in the effects of central class variables on voting choice, 1964 and 1974*

| | Central class variables | | | Effects of other variables | Total |
|---|---|---|---|---|---|
| | Direct effects | Indirect effects | Total | | |
| 1964 totals | 0.184 | 0.203 | 0.387 | | |
| Adjustment for Education* | 0.049 | 0.014 | 0.063 | | |
| Adjustment for Parents' Class† | 0.072 | −0.072 | 0.000 | | |
| | 0.305 | 0.145 | 0.450 | 0.356 | 0.806 |
| Central class % | 67.8 | 32.2 | 100 | | |
| Total % | 37.8 | 18.0 | 55.8 | 44.2 | 100 |
| 1974 totals | 0.100 | 0.184 | 0.284 | | |
| Adjustment for Education* | 0.024 | 0.011 | 0.035 | | |
| Adjustment for Parents' Class† | 0.037 | −0.037 | 0.000 | | |
| | 0.161 | 0.158 | 0.319 | 0.349 | 0.669 |
| Central class % | 50.5 | 49.5 | 100 | | |
| Total % | 24.1 | 23.7 | 47.8 | 52.2 | 100 |

\* These are effects that required the presence of a central class variable in order to become effective (see Table 1).

† These are effects that are properly regarded as direct effects when the two central class variables are considered together, being direct effects of occupation (see Table 1).

What we see in Figure 5.2, therefore, is a model in which class forces contribute more than half (0.450) of total influences (0.806) in 1964, and in which, of this majority influence, 0.305 are direct influences:

[13] The same result would have been obtained in a 'stagewise' regression analysis which took out the effects of central variables before investigating other influences (see Chapter 2).

more than twice the 0.145 of indirect influences flowing via the net-work of supportive social characteristics. It may be a near thing, but clearly this can reasonably be regarded as a model of class voting. Above all, it is a model which finds voting choice firmly anchored in characteristics that were (at least in 1964, see below) not easily changed during adult life. By contrast, housing, education, parental partisanship, even union membership, can be seen to be *incidental* reinforcements to class voting, through the happenstance of class polarization within the milieux in question. It is only their strong links with central variables that give to these supportive variables their powerful reinforcing effects. This contrast may be more easily appreciated if we consider a country such as Australia which has many of the same political features as are found in the British land-scape, but lacks class links with housing tenure for example (McAllister, 1984).

So the model is one which, in 1964, resisted electoral volatility. But because this resistance is partly based on the presumed greater permanence of occupational characteristics as compared with other adult characteristics, it is not something we would have expected to endure in the face of increasing occupational mobility. The divide between working-class and middle-class occupations had always been considered a particularly difficult one to cross. Nevertheless the Oxford Mobility Study has shown that by 1972, far from its being hard to change one's occupational class, this had in fact become one of the most volatile of social characteristics (Heath, 1981).[14] So it should come as no surprise for us to discover that when the accounting operation summarized above is repeated for the 1974 coefficients reported in Figure 5.2, the primacy of central class variables can no longer be documented.

---

[14] Successive studies of voting choice do not provide an ideal means of measuring social mobility because only in the re-interviewing of the same people who are asked anew about their social characteristics does mobility data arise. However, attempts at re-interviewing the same people will fail to find many of those who have moved house. The young and the old will also be under-represented if the waves are fielded several years apart. Nevertheless, our panels of voters can tell us about any *trends* in the extent of social mobility, and analysis of this data confirms that while the trend in occupational mobility was *upwards* during the decade, with mobility per annum between working- and middle-class occupations in 1970–74 up by a quarter of its extent in 1963–66; at the same time the trends in housing tenure and union membership were *downwards*, with some 30 per cent less mobility per annum at the end of the period than at the start.

**The decline of central class influences by 1974**

Table 5.2 summarizes the calculations needed to evaluate the decline in the influence of central class variables by 1974. Clearly these influences had declined considerably during the decade. Not only had the total effects of Parents' Class and Occupation declined by a third to make up only 42 per cent of the much reduced sum of total effects (0.284 out of 0.669), but the increment to these total effects obtainable by claiming credit for the educational influences that pass via occupation (in line with our amendment to the 1964 computations) had declined even more precipitously to a mere 3.5 per cent. So by 1974 this model in which class forces show themselves to best possible advantage could no longer attribute as much as half of the effects on voting choice to central class variables. Instead of dominating by a margin of 0.450 to 0.356, central class variables in 1974 were themselves dominated by a margin of 0.349 to 0.319.

Even more importantly, the table shows that indirect effects were hardly changed over the decade. Such influences as central class variables continued to exert in 1974 are shown in Table 5.2 to be shared almost equally between direct and indirect influences, instead of being very largely direct in nature. Moreover, the continued power of indirect influences arises largely from an increase in the influence of supportive variables (see below). Without this change, the decline in central class influences would have been even more precipitous. The real contrast between the two election years comes in the virtual halving of the direct effects of Parents' Class and Occupation, from 0.305 in 1964 to 0.161 in 1974, while other influences remained largely unchanged (see Table 5.3). As a consequence, the ability of the class system to anchor voting choice in a structure that is relatively resistant to volatile change had been largely eroded. Indeed, the decline in the direct effects of Parents' Class shown in Table 5.3 was greater even than the decline in the direct effects of Occupation, so the change we observe is not simply the inevitable consequence of increasing occupational mobility. The primary implication of the changes we see there is to reinforce the effects of increasing occupational mobility on party choice.

So not only have social characteristics declined in their ability to structure party choice, but such social constraints as remain are more readily altered during adult life. These are characteristics which, moreover, have no inherent influence on voting choice but can serve to

Table 5.3. *Direct effects of central and supportive variables compared for all respondents, 1964 and 1974*

| Effects of | 1964 | 1974 | Change in effect 1964 to 1974 | Change % of 1964 |
|---|---|---|---|---|
| Parents' Class | 0.107 | 0.046 | −0.061 | −57.0 |
| R's Occupation | 0.198 | 0.115 | −0.083 | −41.9 |
| Central | 0.305 | 0.161 | −0.144 | −47.2 |
| Parents' Party | 0.261 | 0.244 | −0.017 | − 6.4 |
| R in Union | 0.087 | 0.099 | +0.012 | +13.8 |
| R's Housing | 0.154 | 0.164 | +0.010 | + 6.5 |
| Supportive | 0.502 | 0.507 | +0.005 | + 1.0 |
| Total effects | 0.807 | 0.668 | | |

transmit and reinforce any political preferences, including those that might turn out to be quite temporary. Of the six variables we have been considering, Parents' Class, Parents' Party, Education, and Occupation were the four that, in 1964, best served to anchor voting choice in an unchangeable mould. Of these only Parents' Party remains today an important determinant of voting choice, and even this is not a variable with a set influence. Inheritance can transmit *any* political preference established for a period long enough to see new voters entering the electorate who had the opportunity during childhood of feeling its effects: a period which might in many cases be as short as four years.

It might be wondered whether the findings presented above arose at least in part from the fact that 1974 saw a dramatic increase in minor party voting, so that for major party voters the effects of central class variables declined less. It is, after all, among major party voters that we would expect to find class forces at their most powerful. But Table 5.4 shows that the decline in the importance of central class variables among major party voters was even more extensive than among all respondents (Table 5.3), with a change in effect of 0.158 compared to 0.144 for the universe comprising all respondents. At the same time, the table makes it clear that the difference between the two universes under examination lay primarily in the behaviour of supportive variables. In the universe comprising all respondents these changed little in their effects between 1964 and 1974, so that the decline of the central variables indexed in Table 5.3 brought with it an overall decline in our ability to predict voting choice of an equivalent amount. In the universe comprising major party voters, by contrast, the decline in the structuring effects of central variables was largely offset by an increase in the structuring effects of supportive variables, leaving a net decline of only 0.044 (0.114 − 0.158).

Table 5.4.  *Total effect of central and supportive variables compared for major party voters, 1964 and 1974*

| Effect of | 1964 | 1974 | Change in effect 1964 to 1974 | Change % of 1964 |
|---|---|---|---|---|
| Parents' Class | 0.169 | 0.115 | −0.054 | −32.0 |
| R's Occupation | 0.241 | 0.137 | −0.104 | −43.2 |
| Central | 0.410 | 0.252 | −0.158 | −38.5 |
| Parents' Party | 0.303 | 0.275 | −0.028 | − 9.2 |
| R in Union | 0.068 | 0.138 | +0.070 | +102.9 |
| R's Housing | 0.173 | 0.245 | +0.072 | +41.6 |
| Supportive | 0.544 | 0.658 | +0.114 | +21.0 |

In particular, two variables which show some gains in structuring voting choice among all respondents show quite dramatic gains among major party voters. Here the effects of housing tenure increase by over 40 per cent, while an equivalent absolute gain on the part of union membership results in a doubling of that variables' rather modest 1964 effect. These increases might reflect in part the increasing importance of housing and union issues as these affect individuals with different characteristics, but this observation only serves to reinforce the incidental nature of the structuring properties of these variables. Should the issues in question lose their salience at some later date, the corresponding social characteristics would lose part of their apparent structuring power as well. At the same time, the increasing importance of these two variables may serve to shed some light on a major paradox that has emerged in recent British voting studies.

### The ecological paradox in British class voting

Almost as well-documented as the *decline* in the power of social class to structure partisanship at the individual level in Britain is the *increase* in the power of class to structure partisanship at the constituency level.

In a seminal article, Miller has demonstrated the existence of a very powerful relationship between the percentage of employers and managers in a constituency and the percentage of votes cast for the Conservative party (Miller, 1978; Curtice and Steed, 1983). In 1964 fully 69 per cent of the variance in Conservative voting figures could be explained by this variable alone, and by 1974 the percentage had increased to a staggering 77 per cent (Miller, 1978, p. 276).[15]

By mathematical manipulation of separately derived survey and constituency estimates for the effects of social class, Miller suggests that there are two effects on class voting. One of these is the individual-level effect which we have been investigating, having to do with the power of a person's own characteristics to determine his or her partisanship. The other is an area effect which has to do with the power of constituency characteristics to determine the partisanship of the individuals who live there. The constituency-level findings point to an increase in the area effect on partisanship corresponding to the decline in the effect of individual characteristics, and Miller suggests that 'the whole system of class polarization may be in a state of dynamically stable equilibrium with self-cancelling trends more likely than anything else' (p. 283). This is because one of the things that can stop the area effect from dominating completely, so that all working-class individuals in a predominantly middle-class constituency end up voting Conservative and vice versa, is the power of individual-level characteristics (p. 281). Conversely, one of the things that can restrict the power of individual characteristics to structure partisanship would be a strong area effect making itself felt on members of the minority class in each constituency.

If this suggestion is correct, then all that may have happened is that one form of class voting in Britain has been replaced by another, and the party system is safe from more radical changes. But is the suggestion correct? It is possible that the increase in the power of

[15] It may not be immediately clear how a variable measured at the constituency level can explain so much of the variance in votes cast when essentially the same variable measured at the individual level can explain little more than 10 per cent of the variance in voting choice (8 per cent in 1974). The problem arises because, at the individual level, someone either votes for a particular party or they do not. They cannot cast a proportion of a vote to match the probability associated with their occupation. On the other hand, in analysing constituency election returns this problem does not arise. At the constituency level, the Labour vote does not have to be (and indeed never is) 100 per cent. So readers should not be overly impressed by the high level of variance explained in the constituency analysis. What *is* important is the different direction of the trend.

constituency class characteristics to structure constituency electoral outcomes may be no more than an ironic concomitant of the decline of class structuring on an individual basis. As the supportive variables in our analysis have come to bear more weight in predicting voting choice, so the class composition of different constituencies will also have become a better predictor of constituency outcomes. This is because patterns of housing tenure, in particular, will have tended to cluster geographically, so that more middle-class constituencies will tend to be characterized by high levels of home-ownership while more working-class constituencies will tend rather to be characterized by council house tenancies. This is an inevitable result of differential housing policies by local authorities over a considerable period.

So, other things being equal, we would expect the increasing importance of supportive variables to show up at the constituency level in terms of increasing correlations between class and constituency voting outcomes: precisely what Miller found.

How can we distinguish between Miller's suggested interpretation of his findings and this interpretation? One way is to link the constituency-level data to characteristics of individuals residing in different constituencies who are members of our samples. This is a complex undertaking, but we shall see in Chapter 6 that analysis of data linked in this way does suggest that Miller's aggregate-level findings have no counterparts at the individual level.[16] That is to say, when we take account of other factors such as class and issue positions, the individuals in our samples are scarcely affected by the class complexion of the constituencies in which they reside, as already asserted in Chapter 1. Moreover, the individual-level relationship between constituency class composition and individual partisanship actually *declined* between 1964 and 1974.

The lack of an individual-level counterpart to Miller's area effect is emphasized if we look at the timing of the various changes that have taken place. Miller found variance explained at the constituency level varying between 68 and 70 per cent from 1964 to 1970, and between 77 and 78 per cent thereafter (Miller, 1978, p. 276). In other words the increase he noted occurred in a single step between 1970 and 1974.

[16] Further analysis of the same data shows that the relationship between housing tenure and constituency complexion increased threefold between 1964 and 1974, from a correlation of 0.055 to 0.176; while the relationship between occupation and constituency complexion fell from 0.212 to 0.190. The small magnitude of these relationships reinforces my general feeling of scepticism for the value of inferences made from aggregate data (see below), but the direction of change reinforces my argument about the likely reason for Miller's findings.

We already saw in Figure 4.10 that, at the individual level, class voting declined also in a single step; but that step occurred not between 1970 and 1974 but during the previous inter-election period, between 1966 and 1970. On the face of it this would contradict Miller's suggestion, since a rise in the area effect did not coincide with a decline in the individual effect and we did not have a system in a state of dynamically stable equilibrium. However, Figure 4.10 is perhaps not the correct point of departure for the comparison. After all, this summarized the effects of all six of our independent variables, and in a highly adjusted fashion at that. Perhaps it would be fairer to Miller's interpretation if we were to look only at the behaviour of those variables most centrally connected with the concept of class voting.

Figure 5.3 traces the changing effects of central class variables over the fifteen-year period of our study (solid lines) for major party voters and all respondents, and shows conclusively that although there was a decline in the structuring effects of these two variables between 1970 and 1974, the major decline for both universes had occurred by 1970.[17] At the same time, Figure 5.3 traces the progress of the two variables whose structuring properties increased over the period, housing and union membership (broken lines). These variables, by contrast with the central class variables, do show an increase coinciding with the rise in the area effect reported by Miller, with small fluctuations before and after easily attributable to the effects of swing.[18]

So the decline in class voting at the individual level cannot simply be viewed as a logical concomitant of its increase at the constituency level, with class-based parties as secure in the new structure of partisanship as they were in the old. On the contrary, the rise in class-based partisanship at the constituency level might be due to nothing more than links between the class complexion of constituencies with different housing policies and the voting behaviour of these constituencies. Evidence for this assertion is circumstantial but persuasive. It does not contradict any of Miller's findings, and runs counter only to his suggestion that self-cancelling trends were more likely than anything

[17] Because of difficulties referred to earlier in defining a single causal model correct for all the elections held during our time period, the analyses reported in Figure 5.3 consist of straightforward predictions of voting choice from all six of our independent variables, including respondent's education. The coefficients for education and parents' party are not reported but remain fairly constant over the period, except for a notable drop in 1970 and revival thereafter.

[18] See Chapter 4 for a discussion of the way in which swing can be expected to affect the estimation of class influences.

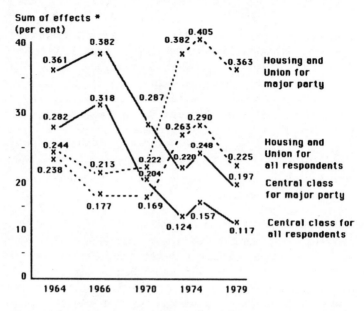

Figure 5.3.   Changes in the effect of social contact and central class
variables in determining voting choice for all respondents
and major party voters, 1964–79*

* These coefficients are partial unstandardized regression estimates from an
analysis in which education was included as a predictor of partisanship. They
are thus not directly comparable with those in Tables 5.2 and 5.5.

else. After all, the area effect was, according to Miller, a matter of social
contacts breeding consensus. Because of the declining importance of
occupational class, the best remaining indicator of politically relevant
social contacts among our six variables must be housing. This has
certainly shown itself increasingly capable of breeding consensus in
recent years, as shown by the rising effect of housing on voting choice.

So it probably does not much matter whether Miller's area effect is
serving as a surrogate for this variable or vice versa. In either case he
would have been right in stressing that electoral politics was becoming
'less and less about "people like me" and more and more about "people
around here"' (Miller, 1978, p. 283). What does matter is our different
prognosis for the future of the British party system. Miller believes that
an increasing local component in voting behaviour could lead to 'a
declining fit to the constituency regressions' (p. 283). The implication

is that this decline would amount to a reduction in class voting which would take place gradually. I would argue that the level of fit to the constituency regressions (the variance they explain) is in fact largely irrelevant to the extent of class voting.

Under my interpretation, Miller's constituency regressions only show a good fit because of the fact that social contacts are transmitting and reinforcing political preferences for the two traditional major parties. But a strong relationship between Conservative voting and the numbers of employers and managers in a constituency could as easily accompany generally low levels of Conservative voting as the generally high levels seen in past elections. So if a particular party loses a large measure of its electoral support, the relationship that continues to exist between support for that party and the class complexion of different constituencies will depend on the rate at which votes for that party are lost in different constituencies. If the rate is fairly similar across the country as a whole, then Miller's correlations will remain high even while support for the party dwindles away.

## Summary and implications

Is class, then, still the basis of British politics? At the individual level the answer must be an unequivocal 'no'. The explanatory power of variables most central to the concept of social class (parents' class and respondent's occupation) had declined so extensively by 1974 that supportive variables which used to reinforce these central influences are now essentially propping up a structure that has lost its backbone. The variables which, at the individual level, have retained their importance are those relating to inherited partisanship and social contacts. Inheritance can transmit any political allegiance from generation to generation, and social contacts can similarly support any type of party system. The contemporary political system consisting of two major parties happens for historical reasons to be class-based, but in elections since 1970 it has been supported only because it is there. Its essential fragility was demonstrated in Scotland by the rapid rise and then decline of Scottish Nationalist partisanship on the part of individuals whose class characteristics should have led them to vote Conservative or Labour.[19] The 1982 surge in by-election voting for the SDP/Liberal alliance was another demonstration of the same fragility.

[19] And the decline was not associated with a ressurgence of class voting, as already shown in Figure 4.10.

At the constituency level research has shown social class to have been rising in importance as a determinant of constituency electoral outcomes, but this appears to be no more than an ironic concomitant of its decline at the individual level. Group processes of opinion formation and dissemination are the props which sustain what is left of the British class vote, but to the extent that class-based voting patterns are sustained in this manner election results come increasingly to be determined by the particular mix of social characteristics found in each constituency. If ever a new alignment springs up, it too is likely to be supported by these same processes, and the high correlations found between class and electoral outcomes at the constituency level may still be seen even under a completely different party system. But the high correlations found between class and electoral support *for any particular party* could vanish just as easily as the much lower correlations between class and voting choice at the individual level. The strength of the relationship is no guarantee of its durability, and neither is the fact that it has risen in recent years.

In terms of Huckfeldt's (1983) view of the social context of political change, the developments described in this chapter moved the British electorate from a predominantly *social group* basis to a predominantly *behavioural contagion* basis for electoral choice. Huckfeldt showed that these two models have similar properties, except that the social group basis has an intrinsic equilibrium to which the system returns after displacement caused conflicting stimuli (such as, in Huckfeldt's example, Watergate). The behavioural contagion model, by contrast,

produces an equilibrium that is constantly redefined by prevailing opinion and mass behaviour, and the return to equilbrium is a never-ending accommodation to a mixture of positive and negative reinforcements that may be highly volatile and rapidly altered (p. 940).

Huckfeldt provides no discussion of the implications of mixing his two models to different extents within the same political system at the same time, but the idea of such a mixture is inherent in the approach taken in this chapter. The change in the basis of electoral choice which we have documented amounts to a change in the relative importance to be ascribed to each model. An electorate operating under a predominantly social group model has no means for long-term change other than changes in the sizes of the social groups resulting from demographic mechanisms. An electorate operating under a behavioural contagion model has the opportunity of undergoing long-term change, although this need not necessarily come about. What we have proposed in this chapter (and will further investigate in Chapter 6) is that the effects of behavioural contagion (which we have called social contacts) are limited by group politics in the shape of class voting. Behavioural contagion only becomes possible to the extent that group politics declines. This is what happened to British politics between 1964 and 1974.

# 6

# THE RISE OF ISSUE VOTING

In past chapters we have established beyond reasonable doubt that a decline has occurred in the extent of British class voting. But if class has declined as a determinant of partisanship, what, if anything, has taken its place?

Unless we can find a satisfactory answer to this question, we will be left in the unfortunate position of having to suspect that voting behaviour may have become less rather than more rational in recent years, with the electorate casting its vote increasingly on the basis of whim and impulse. Happily there is an obvious candidate for successor to class voting whose credentials should be investigated. It seems reasonable to hypothesize that the decline of class voting will have opened the way, at least to a limited extent, for a rise in 'issue voting' (the dependency of voting choice on policy preferences) to take place, and the purpose of the present chapter is to investigate this hypothesis.

Certainly, on the basis of causal observation, issues do seem to have increased in importance in recent years, and respondents to post-election surveys now appear better informed about political issues than they were twenty years ago. Asked to name the important issues that helped them decide how to vote, fewer than 6 per cent of respondents to a series of surveys conducted following recent elections were unable to name a second issue. Twenty years ago 40 per cent of respondents were unable to name as many as two important questions facing the country (see Figure 6.1).

The possibility that the declining salience of social class within the British electorate has removed a constraint that used to hamper issue voting constitutes an attractive hypothesis, but there is an alternative possibility which would be a great deal more prosaic. This is that class voting is still with us, though in a different guise. This second hypothesis was suggested by Miller (1978) who has demonstrated, as we saw in Chapter 5, that the class composition of different constituencies, as measured by the proportion of employers and managers in each, has increased as a determinant of constituency election results even as individual class characteristics have declined as determinants of individual

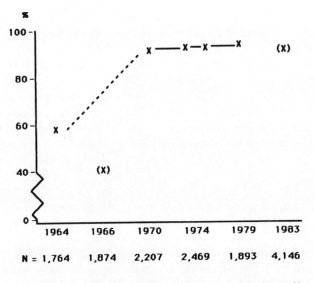

Figure 6.1.   Ability to think of more than one important problem
facing the country, all respondents 1964–83

voting choice. However, aggregate studies of this kind can easily run
foul of the ecological fallacy which occurs when relationships found
between geographic areas are assumed to apply to the characteristics
which typify those areas.[1] Such studies must therefore be treated
with considerable caution. Although Kramer (1983) has recently shown
that individual-level findings are also subject to bias, and may indeed
yield less reliable estimates than aggregate-level findings in certain
circumstances, the most important lesson to be drawn from Kramer's
work is that ecological- and individual-level analyses can generally be
reconciled. Each form of analysis will then shed light on a different
aspect of the social processes concerned.

---

[1]  The classic example of an ecological fallacy was that which linked race and
literacy in the United States (Robinson, 1956). Southern states had large proportions of blacks in their populations, and also large proportions of illiterates
compared with other states. It was easy to conclude from this that blacks tended
to be illiterate, but such a conclusion turned out to be false: in southern states
even whites had very high rates of illiteracy, and the differences between blacks
and whites were much less than the differences between states.

Indeed, Miller's findings are by no means incompatible with our own hypothesis. It is quite possible that increasing effects from social milieu have gone along with increasing importance of issues, in which case it will be necessary to attempt to determine whether one of these influences is merely a spurious concomitant of the other. In order to guard against this possibility, the present chapter also investigates the impact of social milieu, as measured by the proportion of employers and managers in the constituency in which each individual resides, on the voting behaviour of those individuals.

## The data

In this chapter we supplement our social structure variables in several ways. In the first place we add a number of variables representing the importance of issues whose nature is discussed below. In the second place one variable was added from another source entirely. This measured the proportion of employers and managers among inhabitants of the constituency in which each respondent was resident at the time of the election concerned. For the elections of 1964 and 1966 this and other census variables had already been added to the survey data in the course of the Strathclyde Historical Elections Project (Miller, 1977). For the elections of 1970 to 1979 the variable was added to each data set as part of the research conducted for the present study.[2]

In the third place, two dependent variables have been employed. One of these, Voting Choice, is the same as that used in past chapters, derived from the 'How did you vote' question in each of the surveys by dichotomizing supporters of the Labour party against the rest.[3] The other is a measure of party identification derived from the

[2] This chapter is based on an article entitled 'Assessing the Rise of Issue Voting in British Elections since 1964', published in *Electoral Studies* in 1985. I am grateful to Butterworths, the publishers, for allowing me to make use of material employed there. The lengthy and intricate procedure of matching up constituency identification numbers, specifying the correspondences, sorting and weighting the correspondence lists, and then merging two data sets on the basis of the matched identification numbers was performed by Ann Mair of the University of Strathclyde Social Statistics Laboratory, for whose patient assistance I am greatly indebted.

[3] The use of Conservative vs. rest as a dependent variable makes little difference to our findings. It simply has the effect of understating the effect of class voting, and emphasizing the rise in the importance of issues. Because we seek to establish the importance of issue voting in this study, we prefer to use the more conservative basis for measurement.

question, 'Generally speaking, do you usually think of yourself as . . .?' Again this was dichotomized to distinguish supporters of the Labour party from others. This variable was included so that we could confront the problem of how far issue preferences are contaminated by party identification (see next section).

Party identification is a concept particularly appropriate to the study of American voting behaviour since Americans have traditionally registered an identification with a party that is quite separate from (though correlated with) their voting choice. In Britain there has been controversy over the meaningfulness of this concept considering that voter registration does not involve any question of party identification, and that voters questioned on the subject are likely to answer with the name of the party they most recently voted for. However, British political scientists are coming to increasingly value the concept in an era of electoral volatility (Alt, Crewe, and Sarlvik, 1977), and we will see that it works well in the context of our present concerns.

Except for Tables 1 and 2, all analyses reported in this chapter exclude non-voters but included minor party voters along with those who voted Conservative or Labour.

## The problem of issue voting

The study of issue voting is complicated by a number of factors, some of which are discussed at length in Butler and Stokes (1974, pp. 277 ff).[4] In particular, it is not at all clear to what extent issue preferences are independent of party identification. On the contrary, considerable evidence has been amassed over the years to support the proposition that issue preferences are mediated by party preference. The classic solution to this problem is that pioneered by V. O. Key Jr. in his study of the *Responsible Electorate* (Key, 1966) which is to look at the issue preferences of those members of the electorate who switched from support of one party to support of another since the time of the previous election. The rationale for this procedure, though never supported by hard evidence, is that 'switchers' (as Key called them) are those least likely to have their issue preferences contaminated by long-standing party identification. We will employ this procedure ourselves in the next section in order to establish the rise of issue voting

---

[4] The problem of issue voting has been widely discussed in the American literature on voting behaviour. A good but not very recent bibliography is to be found in Margolis (1977).

in this context during our period. However, this solution does not permit the sort of multivariate analysis which is necessary in order to distinguish the effects of issue preferences from those of class and social milieu. For the latter purpose we need to be able to build a causal model in which the effects of issue preferences are measured for the whole electorate and not just those who switched parties.

The measurement of issue preferences is itself a vexed question. Butler and Stokes (1974, pp. 290–5) suggest that there are three conditions which should be fulfilled before an issue can be expected to affect an electoral outcome. The first is that the issue should be *salient*, the second that it should be *integrated* into the party system, with one party being perceived as opposing the other on the issue, and the third that opinions should be *skewed* in such a way that one party gains an electoral advantage from the position it takes. Meier and Campbell (1979) add that the voters should *correctly perceive* the issue positions taken by each party. When we are concerned with the effects of issues on the voting choice of individuals (as distinct from the electorate as a whole), we can ignore the third requirement of skewedness, and the question of salience becomes one that has to be answered for each individual separately. The requirement of correct perception is perhaps a little strong. It is, of course, of the greatest importance that party stances *as perceived by each voter* be employed rather than party stances as perceived by the investigator (Page and Jones, 1979, p. 1073). And certainly it would be desirable that issue voting were based on correct perception of party positions, but perceptions could influence voting decisions even though they were incorrect. However, in so far as it is possible to verify the 'correctness' of political preferences among our respondents, they appear remarkably competent to perceive party stances correctly.[5]

With these points in mind we can construct an index measuring the extent of issue-based support for any political party by establishing, for each of a number of issues, the extent to which each respondent considers it a salient issue, the position he takes on that issue, and the identity of the party (if any) which he views as taking the same

[5] For many issues the 'best party' to achieve a given objective would be a matter of opinion, but each year there are at least some issue postures which can be unambiguously credited to one party or another. These range from four in 1964 to nine in October 1974. On these issues only some 10 per cent of respondents on average misperceived the party most likely to pursue a particular policy, with a high of 13 per cent in 1970, and a low of 6 per cent in each of the 1974 elections. This statistic shows no discernible trend over our time period.

position. Issue-based preference for a party could then be calculated by taking a simple sum of the number of times that party is preferred with regard to important issues. Unfortunately, changes in questionnaire design over the years mean that we cannot establish these three things in precisely the same manner for each of the elections with which we are concerned. In 1966 and 1970 we have comparable variables in almost all respects: a multiple response item measuring issue import-ance, a set of questions measuring positions on specific issues, and a corresponding set measuring perceived party postures on the same issues. In 1964 we have everything in this list except the multiple-response items measuring issue importance. However, we do have the items in question measured for most of the 1964 sample in a previous wave of the same panel study, in 1963, and (for some issues) an inde-pendent check on the consistency of these items with 1964 feelings of issue importance.[6]

From 1974 to 1979 we have a rather different measure of salience, in that respondents were asked whether each issue was important to them or not, rather than, as in previous years, being asked simply to list important issues which might or might not include those for which specific questions as to attitude and party postures would then be asked. So in these later studies more of the issues for which we have attitude and party posture data emerge as salient than in earlier studies, and there is a much greater degree of variation between different respondents on the number of respects in which they prefer their most preferred party. So the resulting indices of issue-based party preferences

[6] In both 1964 and 1966 separate questions were asked about strength of respondent feeling about immigration, and about the seriousness of strikes. On the multiple response item about issue importance both these issues come up again. Thus it is possible to compare consistency in 1966 over these two issues with consistency between 1963 and 1964 over the same two issues, as is done in the table below, which gives the percentage of those mentioning the issue as important who also thought it serious (for strikes) or had strong feelings (for immigration).

|  | 1966 consistency (%) | 1963–4 consistency (%) |
|---|---|---|
| Immigration (strong feelings) | 76.0 | 76.3 |
| Strikes (considered serious) | 81.9 | 91.3 |

In both cases, consistent responses to the two questions were in fact more apparent between the 1963 and 1964 waves than within the 1966 wave of the panel study. If this degree of consistency is representative of what would have been found for other issues in the 1964 questionnaire, then we would have no qualms about using 1963 measures of issue importance in conjunction with other variables from 1964.

had to be normalized on the basis of the number of issues each respondent considered salient.

Finally, in 1983 the Gallup surveys employ yet a third means of measuring issue influence which has more in common with earlier post-election studies than with those of 1974 and 1979.

Whether our indices of issue-based party support are in fact comparable from year to year is a question that cannot easily be resolved; but the fact that the measures are almost completely identical for the two elections of 1966 and 1970, and for the three elections of 1974 and 1979, gives us some firm ground upon which we can build in considering whether any trends we may discern are at least plausible.

### The rise of issue voting in British elections

Issue voting can be viewed at two levels. At the level of the electorate as a whole, for issue voting to have non-random consequences requires a polarization of party preferences with regard to certain issues, so that there is widespread agreement as to which party should be preferred by those with particular issue concerns. At the individual level it requires that people vote in accordance with these widespread perceptions.

Considering the level of the electorate first, Table 6.1 shows the degree of correlation between our indices of issue-based party preference (described above) and the individual issues from which the indices were constructed. This shows clearly that while in 1964 few issues correlated well with Pro-Labour or Pro-Conservative preferences, indicating that different individuals based their party preferences on different issue concerns, by 1983 issue-based party preferences had become much more polarized in terms of many more issues. The columns of Table 6.1 contain only three coefficients above 0.2 for 1964, when the eighteen coefficients average 0.035. For 1983, by contrast, the columns contain ten coefficients over 0.2, and the eighteen coefficients concerned average 0.219. The lack of polarization of issues in 1964 is emphasized by the fact that three issues were positively correlated with issue-based preferences for both parties. By 1983 there were no such issues, and the high correlations observed in 1983 were already visible in earlier elections (see Table 2.5).

Equally, at the individual level, viewed in a simple-minded fashion in terms of voting in accord with issue-based party preferences, it is clear that issue voting increased between 1964 and 1983. If we start by taking the index of issue-based preference for the Labour party, and

Table 6.1.  *Correlations (Pearson's r) between issue-based party choice and various issue positions, for all respondents, 1964 and 1983\**

|  | 1964 | | 1983 | |
| --- | --- | --- | --- | --- |
|  | RPL | RPC | RPL | RPC |
| Government economic involvement | 0.156 | −0.019 | 0.192 | −0.204 |
| Nationalization/privatization | 0.285 | −0.242 | 0.240 | −0.322 |
| Defence and foreign affairs | 0.044 | −0.084 | 0.368 | −0.406 |
| European community | 0.026 | −0.066 | 0.271 | −0.229 |
| Education | 0.118 | 0.009 | 0.110 | −0.129 |
| Tough on crime, unions, morals, etc. | 0.054 | −0.103 | 0.290 | −0.372 |
| Housing | 0.262 | 0.038 | | |
| Transport | 0.048 | 0.037 | | |
| Immigration | 0.012 | −0.097 | | |
| Proportional representation | | | 0.041 | −0.087 |
| Government should negotiate | | | 0.175 | −0.184 |
| Government should compromise | | | 0.051 | −0.238 |

\* RPL = Respondent Pro Labour on issues.
  RPC = Respondent Pro Conservative on issues.

*Sources:*  Butler and Stokes 1963–1964 election studies. Gallup 1983 election study. Variables were grouped in such a way as to maximize comparability between the two studies. This left three issues from 1964 not matched by corresponding 1983 issues, and so three issues were chosen representative of remaining 1983 issues to create a comparable set. The variables RPC and RPL were generated from all issues available in each year, not grouped in any way.

correlate this with Labour voting in 1964 and 1983, we find that the Pearsonian correlation increases from 0.418 in 1964 to 0.771 in 1983. The correlation of the corresponding Conservative index with Conservative voting increased even more, from 0.328 to 0.797, so that by 1983 issue-based preference was explaining some 63 per cent of the variance in Conservative voting. However, these studies at the extreme ends of our time period are not comparable in a number of respects. Not only is comparability of the data in some doubt because they were collected for different purposes and at different times in relation to the elections concerned (see Chapter 3), but also any findings deriving from these data will be subject to bias because the electoral balance of the parties was not the same (see Chapter 5). A better match for 1964 is February 1974, in which the corresponding correlation was 0.713.

Turning next to whether those who switch parties do so on issue grounds, Table 6.2(a) compares the average of issue-based preferences for the Labour party on the part of those switching to a Labour vote with the average among those remaining committed to the Conservative party between 1959 and 1964, and between 1970 and 1974. It shows that the difference between switchers and non-switchers is much greater in the second of the two election pairs. Between 1970 and 1974 those who switched parties were much more likely to have issue-based preferences for the party they switched to than between 1964 and 1966, as

Table 6.2(a).  *Average extent of issue-based preferences for the Labour Party among switchers and non-switchers from Conservative, 1959-64 and 1970-74*

|  | 1959–1964 | 1970–1974 |
|---|---|---|
| Voted Con in both elections | 0.512 (N=579) | 0.498 (N=603) |
| Voted Con in first election, Lab in second | 0.592 (N= 99) | 0.719 (N=148) |
| Difference of Means* | 0.080 | 0.221 |

Table 6.2(b).  *Average extent of issue-based preferences for the Conservative Party among switchers and non-switchers from Labour, 1959-64 and 1970-74†*

|  | 1959–1964 | 1970–1974 |
|---|---|---|
| Voted Lab in both elections | 0.416 (N=487) | 0.427 (N=861) |
| Voted Lab in first election, Con in second | 0.646 (N= 28) | 0.865 (N= 73) |
| Difference of Means* | 0.230 | 0.438 |

† Except in this analysis, the Conservative index is set to decline with increasing conservatism so as to give positive values when predicting Labour voting choice.

* Using a composite index of issue based party preference embodying both of the indices employed in this table, and decomposing the variance in this index across categories of consistent and inconsistent voting in 1964 and 1974, switching explains 23.6 per cent of variance in 1964. By 1974 variance explained in the corresponding index had more than doubled to 58.6 per cent.

shown by the difference of means (last row of the subtable). Table 6.2(b) does the same for voters switching to Conservative.

But these perspectives on issue voting are much too simple-minded to be of much use. In the first place, they skirt the question of whether issue-based preferences reflect rather than cause a prior decision on how to vote, and in the second place (rather more subtly) they ignore the fact that issue-based preferences may themselves be partial consequences of prior influences (for example, from early socialization or social status). Reference to American voting studies emphasizes the possible importance of these influences.

### Towards a model of issue-based voting in British elections

Goldberg (1966) proposed a model of class and issue voting that is particularly suitable as a starting point for our purposes. It made issue-based preferences dependent in part on party identification which was in turn dependent on class and socializing influences, as illustrated in Figure 6.2. This model, which we shall call Model A, was proposed after previous analysis had rejected two alternative models positing, on the one hand, a funnelling of causation through issue preferences and, on the other hand, its funnelling through party identification. The revised model gave a good fit to data on voting behaviour in the 1956 American election, except that a direct effect on Issue Preferences was found to come from Parents' Social Class, reflecting a continuing influence of early socialization. The model attempts to overcome the problem of issue preferences reflecting party identification by separating out party identification from the vote decision and positing that the latter is partially determined by issue-based party preferences (which Goldberg terms 'political attitudes'), which in turn are partially determined by party identification.

In order to apply this model to our British data, we had to combine the two issue-based indices of party choice that were used in Table 6.2 and earlier into a single measure of Respondent's Political Attitudes (RPA). This was done by subtracting the Conservative index from the Labour index to yield a measure that could be negative or positive depending on the party preferred on balance.

We already explained Party Identification in the section on data. Respondent's Social Characteristics is the other variable appearing in the model that may require some explanation. Goldberg is in fact concerned with the same three adult socializing forces (occupation,

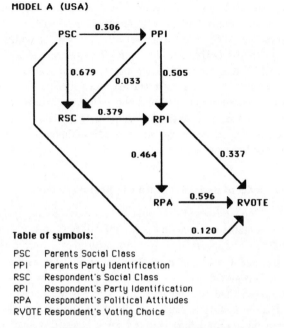

**MODEL A (USA)**

Figure 6.2.   Goldberg's proposed model of voting behaviour in
American presidential elections, with an additional path
discovered empirically (PSC to RVOTE) and
coefficients for 1956

*Source:* Adapted from Model III in Goldberg (1966).

union membership, and housing) as we have been concerned with in
previous chapters. However, incorporating all three of these influences
into the model would create considerable problems simply in terms of
drawing all the linkages, and even more in terms of analysing the data.
So he computed an index from the three variables which best summarized their causal influence on voting choice.[7]

Applied to British voting data from the elections of 1964 to 1979,
Goldberg's model (Model A) also does quite well, although in our case

---

[7] The additive index Respondent's Social Class was derived from the three
dichotomies for Respondent's Occupation, Home Ownership, and Union Membership by employing regression analysis to derive the equation that best predicts
party choice from these three variables. For each respondent, the value of RSC is
the best prediction of Labour Voting Choice that can be made from the regression
equation. This is identical to the procedure employed by Goldberg in deriving his
corresponding index (Goldberg, 1966).

we find no significant influence from Parents' Class to Respondent's Political Attitudes. Instead we find small but sometimes statistically significant influences from Respondent's Social Class both to Respondent's Attitudes and to his Voting Choice. These influences are at their greatest in the election of 1966, whose coefficients are those illustrated in Figure 6.3.[8]

The illustration shows that the direct effects of Respondent's Political Attitudes on voting choice was 0.129, only some 13 per cent of the total effect on 1966 voting choice, most of which came from Party Identification (see Table 6.3). Moreover, the coefficients on the paths leading in to Respondent's Political Attitudes indicate that this variable was itself largely determined by prior influences (0.101 + 0.416 = 0.517). In 1966, it seems, voters' perceptions of party stances were largely coloured by their own class and especially by their party identification. Thus any balanced view of the independent contribution of issue preferences to voting choice has to subtract transmitted influences of some 7 per cent (the product of 0.101 × 0.129 plus the product of 0.416 × 0.129).[9] Table 6.3 summarizes the gross and net effects of issue-based party preferences on voting choice estimated on the basis of Model A, for all years 1964 to 1983, and shows that on the basis of this model, far from an increase in issue voting between 1964 and 1979, what we find is negligible issue voting at any time.

But is Model A a plausible model of British voting behaviour? In the American context, the relatively small influence of Respondent's Party Identification on Voting Choice (0.337 in Figure 6.2), together

---

[8] The coefficients are beta weights derived from multiple regression analysis which treats each variable (except Parents' Social Class) as dependent in turn on all those variables prior in causal sequence. Beta weights are used in preference to unstandardized regression coefficients because two variables, Respondent's Political Attitudes and Respondents Social Characteristics, are additive indices whose range of values is not comparable with that of the other variables, all of which are dichotomies. However, the interpretation of these coefficients remains much the same as in previous chapters (see Chapter 1). A major drawback in the use of these coefficients for comparisons over time lies in the fact that their values depend on the extent of variation in dependent and independent variables which may differ from data set to data set quite independently of any real difference in the effects we want to measure (Hanushek and Jackson, 1977, p. 78). In order to guard against the possibility of being misled in this way, the models reported in this chapter were all first estimated using unstandardized regression coefficients. The resulting models gave identical results in terms of timing and extent of change, but were less easily interpretable in terms of the relative impact of component variables.

[9] For a description of the manner in which indirect effects can be manipulated and interpreted see Chapters 1 and 5.

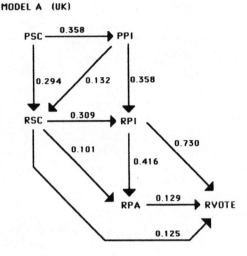

Symbols as for Figure 6.2

Figure 6.3.   A tentative model of British voting behaviour, with additional paths discovered empirically (RSC to RPA and RSC to RVOTE) and coefficients for all voters, 1966

with the relatively large direct effect of Attitudes (0.595) means that any reciprocal causation between Attitudes and Identification would only make a modest difference to the overall effect of Attitudes on Voting Choice.[10] But in the British context the reverse is the case, and even a modest effect of Attitudes on Party Identification would make a very large relative difference to the apparent overall effect of Attitudes.

That there is an effect from attitudes to partisanship has been shown in the American context by Meier and Campbell (1979) who use panel data (repeated re-interviews during a political campaign) to calculate reciprocal effects of Voting Choice on Attitudes and of Attitudes on

[10] For example, if we assume an effect of Attitudes on Identification of one third the magnitude of the effect in the other direction (see below), then the increment given to the overall effect of Attitudes would only be 0.047 = (0.337) X (0.464/3). If we assume the ratio to be two to one rather than three to one, then the increment comes out at 0.078. Nevertheless, to omit the possibility of reciprocal causation between party identification and issue-based party preferences is clearly wrong, even in America, as pointed out by Page and Jones (1979, p. 1078).

Table 6.3. *Gross and net effects of political attitudes on voting choice, both direct and indirect, estimated from Model A for 1964-83*

|  | 1964 | 1966 | 1970 | 1974* | 1979 | 1983 |
|---|---|---|---|---|---|---|
| Direct effects of RPA $(a)$ | 0.086 | 0.129 | 0.128 | 0.149 | 0.244 | –† |
| Effects of RSC on RPA $(b)$ | 0.067 | 0.101 | 0.025 | 0.108 | 0.111 | –† |
| Effects of RPI on RPA $(c)$ | 0.412 | 0.416 | 0.405 | 0.677 | 0.654 | –† |
| Transmitted $(ab+ac)$ $(d)$ | 0.041 | 0.067 | 0.055 | 0.117 | 0.187 | –† |
| Net effects $(a-d)$ $(e)$ | 0.045 | 0.062 | 0.073 | 0.032 | 0.057 | (0.061) |

Symbols as in Model A.

* Figures for 1974 are averages of those obtained for each of the two election studies conducted in that year.

† Calculations for 1983 not comparable because of different question formats and different available variables. Final figure computed by employing 1979 Gallup election surveys as a means of calibration, and correcting the 1983 figure on this basis.

Voting Choice.[11] The second of these effects was estimated at between 0.09 and 0.11, while the first was estimated consistently over three measurements at almost exactly three times this amount, between 0.26 and 0.33. This is admittedly not quite the reciprocal relationship we would have wished to see calculated for our purposes, since we are interested in reciprocal causation between Attitudes and Party Identification rather than between Attitudes and Voting Choice. However, the result is at least suggestive of such a reciprocal relationship, and if we take advantage of the fact that any influence of Parents Party Identification on Respondent's Attitudes must (according to our model) arise indirectly through Respondents Social Class or Respondent's Party

[11] The model developed by Page and Jones (1979) is in many ways closer to our own, but is rendered non-comparable by its inclusion of candidate evaluations in addition to issue evaluations. In the American context candidate evaluations are clearly important and have to be taken into account in any analysis of the determinants of voting choice. In Britain candidate evaluations may be important but cannot readily be taken into account because of fundamental ambiguities inherent in voting choice in a Parliamentary regime. Who is the candidate in a British General Election? Some voters may view the prospective Member of Parliament as the candidate for whom they cast their votes while others may view the leader of the party as the potential Prime Minister for whom they are voting. Faced with this ambiguity, many British voters may well regard the candidate as the political party that encompasses both potential MP and potential PM, and this is the view subsumed by our model. Considerable research would be necessary before it would be possible to construct a model that took candidate evaluations more specifically into account in British voting choice.

Identification, then it is possible to arrive at an algebraic result for the effect of Respondent's Party Identification on his Attitudes and vice versa.[12]

When we perform these calculations for the elections from 1964 to 1979 we do not initially find a consistent ratio between the two reciprocal causal paths, although the path from Party Identification to Attitudes is always the greater of the two.[13] Our next elaboration of the voting behaviour model will find such consistency (see below) at a ratio of about two-to-one, so Model B is presented in Figure 6.4 with coefficients derived from the election of 1970, in which the two-to-one ratio between effects *on* attitudes and effects *of* attitudes came closest to being established.

The first thing to notice about this model is that, as suggested above, the indirect effects of even quite modest influences on party identification from political attitudes can be considerable. Table 4 estimates these effects, and then calculates the net effects of attitudes in the same manner as was done in Table 6.3. As can be seen, Model B produces net attitude effects that are quite respectable, and even show a modest rate of increase over the period. But differences between the nature of American politics in 1956 and British politics twenty years later suggests that even this model may be defective in at least one important respect. A single measure of political attitudes does not allow for the fact that disenchantment with the potential of one political party may not be matched by enchantment with the potential of the other. Respondents may have issue-based preferences for both political parties at the same time, or for neither. In particular, the latter possibility would appear to be one for which we should make allowance when

---

[12] Simple-mindedly, this can be done by saying that the effect of PPI on RPA controlling fro RSC (which is calculable from the data) must be the product of the effect of PPI on RPI controlling for RSC (calculable) and that of RPI on RPA controlling for RSC (unknown). Having computed one of the unknowns in this fashion the other could be derived by algebraic manipulation. See Franklin (1985, note 14) for more details.

[13] Unfortunately we cannot perform these calculations for 1983, since the Gallup surveys do not contain a measure of parental partisanship, or any other suitable instrumental variable for disentangling the problem of reciprocal causation. So we have to take advantage of the fact that transmitted effects are found to be very consistent over our period (see below) in order to estimate total effects of issues in 1983. Even then, correction is necessary for the different manner in which the Gallup data were collected. This was done by computing total effects of issues from 1979 Gallup surveys and comparing these with our own findings for 1979. This gave us a 'calibration error' which could be applied to the 1983 results.

MODEL B

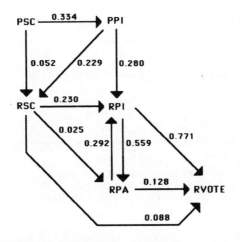

**Symbols as for Figure 6.2.**

Figure 6.4.   A second tentative model of British voting behaviour with reciprocal causation between Party identification and Political attitudes, and coefficients for all voters, 1970

respondents have the option of voting for a party other than Conservative or Labour, and our analyses do include minor party voters even though we have not estimated their issue preferences.[14]

With these considerations in mind, Figure 6.5 presents Model C which differs from Model B in providing two measures of issue-based party preference rather than the one measure required by Goldberg's model. So in this model, Respondent's Political Attitudes have been recast as our original variables Respondent Pro-Labour and Respondent Pro-Conservative, and the layout has been somewhat rearranged in order to accommodate the extra linkages. The model does not perform

[14] Minor party voting will count as issue voting in our analyses to the extent that minor party voters view both of the major parties negatively in terms of issues. Separate analyses of Gallup data show that this was indeed the major issue stance of Alliance voters in 1983. However, positive issue evaluations of minor party stances do not count in our analyses, so it is possible that we still understate the extent of issue voting in those elections when minor parties did well. However, see Lemieux (1977, especially p. 337) for an indication that those who voted Liberal in February 1974 on the basis of issues may not have correctly perceived the Liberal Party's position on those issues.

Table 6.4.  *Gross and net effects of political attitudes on voting choice, both direct and indirect, estimated from Model B for 1964–1983*

|  | 1964 | 1966 | 1970 | 1974* | 1979 | 1983 |
|---|---|---|---|---|---|---|
| Direct effects of RPA (*a*) | 0.086 | 0.129 | 0.128 | 0.149 | 0.244 | –† |
| Indirect via RPI (*b*) | 0.219 | 0.215 | 0.225 | 0.277 | 0.282 | –† |
| Total effects (*a+b*) (*c*) | 0.305 | 0.344 | 0.353 | 0.426 | 0.525 | –† |
| Includes effects** (*d*) | 0.055 | 0.087 | 0.081 | 0.151 | 0.241 | –† |
| Net effects (*c–d*) (*e*) | 0.250 | 0.257 | 0.272 | 0.276 | 0.284 | (0.303) |

† Coefficients for 1983 non-comparable. See Table 6.3.
\* Average of effects in two 1974 elections.
** Sum of paths RSC, RPA, RVOTE + RPI, RPA, RVOTE + RSC, RPA, RPI, RVOTE

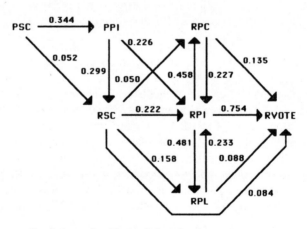

MODEL C

Symbols as for Figure 6.2, except

RPC = Respondent Pro-Conservative on issues
RPL = Respondent Pro-Labour on issues

Figure 6.5.   Proposed model of British voting behaviour with reciprocal causation and dual attitude measurement, and with coefficients for all voters, 1970

much better than Model B in terms of explaining variance in Voting Choice. Largely because of the powerful impact of Party Identification, both models explain some 76 per cent of the variance in 1970, with the more complex model explaining an additional half of one percentage point. However, the additional paths provided for the indirect effects of issue-based preferences can make a lot of difference to the apparent impact of these Attitude variables, and do so especially from 1970 onwards, as can be seen in Table 6.5 which provides the same information as Table 6.4, but for the more elaborate Model C.

In this table for the first time we see a progressive increase in the total effect of issues, by 5 per cent or more per general election, from a low of 0.389 in 1964 to a high of 0.632 in 1979. However, the proportion of this total effect which is properly attributable back in causal sequence to Class and Party Identification (because of the dominant influence of these characteristics on issue perceptions) also varies from year to year, in such a way as to give greater net effects of issues in

Table 6.5.  *Gross and net effects of political attitudes on voting choice, both direct and indirect, estimated from Model C for 1964–1983*

|  | 1964 | 1966 | 1970 | 1974* | 1979 | 1983 |
|---|---|---|---|---|---|---|
| Direct effects of RPC+RPL (*a*) | 0.111 | 0.170 | 0.223 | 0.249 | 0.280 | –† |
| Indirect effects via RPI (*b*) | 0.278 | 0.271 | 0.350 | 0.326 | 0.352 | –† |
| Total effects of RPC+RPL (*c*) | 0.389 | 0.441 | 0.573 | 0.575 | 0.632 | –† |
| Prior effects included** (*d*) | 0.134 | 0.167 | 0.156 | 0.230 | 0.247 | –† |
| Net effects of issues (*e*) | 0.256 | 0.274 | 0.417 | 0.345 | 0.385 | (0.410) |
| Per cent of all effects*** | 25.8 | 26.7 | 39.1 | 36.3 | 40 .1 | (39.6) |

† Calculations for 1983 non-comparable, see Table 6.3.
* Average effects of two 1974 elections.
** Using the same logic as described in note ** to Table 6.4.
*** Total effects of all variables taken together varied slightly, from 0.959 in 1979 to 1.067 in 1970. These differences corresponded to differences in variance explained running from 69.3 per cent to 76.2 per cent in the same two studies. The final row attempts to take account of these overall variations by looking at the extent to which issues contribute to the total of all effects on voting choice.

1970 than in any later year. But the major implication of Table 6.4 is that issue voting rose suddenly between 1966 and 1970, with smaller fluctuations thereafter.

## Class constraints on issue voting

Whatever one may feel about the propriety of algebraic manipulation of regression coefficients in order to untangle the problem of reciprocal causation between political attitudes and party identification, it is virtually certain that some reciprocal causation does take place. In Model C we find this to be very consistent from election to election, with Party Identification having about twice the impact on issue-based party preference that the latter has on Party Identification, as shown in Table 6.5. Even if we are for some reason overestimating the effect of issues on Party Identification, it is implausible that this effect should be less than half what we have estimated, in which case, feeding through the indirect paths in Model C and adding the direct effects of issues will still give us a low of 0.250 and high of 0.391 in the total effect of issues before deduction of (much reduced) transmitted effects. At any level of indirect effects, the general pattern observed in Table 6.5 seems likely to hold good because it is dominated by the direct effects of issue-based preferences. Indirect effects remained remarkably constant throughout the period, with a single step up in 1970 (row *b*).

The fact that this pattern of rise and fall in the effects of issue voting roughly reciprocates the pattern of fall and rise in the corrected effects of class voting (Chapter 4) is suggestive of a possible relationship between issue-based voting choice and class-structured voting, where the level of one is constrained by the level of the other, so that when class voting is high issue voting is necessarily low, and the reverse is also true (see Figure 6.6).

But while the correspondence shown in Figure 6.6 is striking, it must be emphasized that both of the trends depicted there are highly corrected for contaminating influences, and these corrections are quite different in each case. If we knew that there should be an inverse relationship between issue voting and class-based voting, then the reciprocal relationship illustrated in Figure 6.6 would serve to validate both the decontamination procedure employed in Chapter 4 and also the causal model depicted in Figure 6.5. As things stand, we can certainly say that it is highly unlikely that the degree of correspondence seen in Figure 6.6 would have arisen by chance, so that the

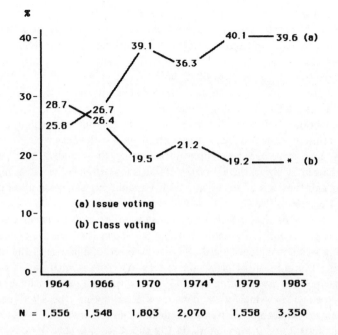

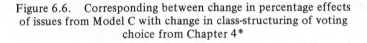

* Decline of class voting taken from Figure 4.10 which contains no coefficient for 1983. Increase in issue voting taken from Table 6.5, bottom row.

† Average of two elections for 1974.

Figure 6.6. Corresponding between change in percentage effects of issues from Model C with change in class-structuring of voting choice from Chapter 4*

correspondence adds verisimilitude to our procedures, and also suggests that class voting and issue voting are indeed inversely related.

A second indirect test of this hypothesis can be conducted if we return to our data from the election of 1964. If issue voting at that election was being held down by class influences, then we should find greater issue voting among those respondents least consistently affected by class influences: those whose class characteristics cut across each other rather than reinforcing each other. In Chapter 4 an index was constructed which measured the number of characteristics (out of six) that each respondent possessed which were typical of a working-class social upbringing and environment. If we select for analysis only those individuals (about two thirds of the sample) who had between two and four such characteristics, we will remove from consideration those whose characteristics were prototypically working class or middle class. If we then repeat the analysis reported in Table 6.5 for these individuals, the results are most illuminating. Total effects of issues in 1964 for those in mixed-class strata were considerably higher than for the sample as a whole at 0.498, though not as high as in later years. However, because only a small part of these effects could be attributed to the prior influence of class (transmitted prior influences were necessarily low since we were only investigating those individuals least influenced by class), the net effect of issues for these people was as high as at any time in our study, at 0.394. Variance explained was also high at 74 per cent.

This lack of class effects to be transmitted forwards by issues is also a feature of our 1970 findings. Table 6.5 shows that the rise of issue voting was not matched until 1974 by a corresponding rise in the off-setting transmission of class effects (row *d*). This is what gave us an initial peak in issue voting for 1970. Now that we have documented the manner in which class constrains issue voting, the 1970 peak becomes explicable in terms of demographic trends in the social characteristics of British voters. In Chapter 4 we saw how the number of respondents in cross-pressured (or ambiguous) class situations rose to a high point in 1970, only to decline again four years later. The number of respondents who might have been expected to be most constrained by class characteristics was therefore at its very lowest in 1970, accentuating the apparent rise of issue voting in that year.

So it would appear safe to conclude that reducing class constraints on voting choice had something to do with the rise of issue voting, given our 1970 findings. For if the high extent of issue voting in that year is attributable partly to demographic considerations, demography would clearly be independent of any general public mood or fashion that favoured issue voting. So circumstantial evidence points to the causal priority of declining class voting in accounting for the rise of issue voting that we have documented in past pages. Figure 6.6 does show a greater rise in issue voting than it shows decline in class voting, but this is because the two trends are measured in different ways for different purposes, and hence appear on different scales. If the effects of class are measured by summing the total effects attributable to class in our models, in the same manner as we have measured the total effects of issue voting, then the decline turns out to be of comparable magnitude to the rise in the effects of issues. The only other component in our model which has any direct influence on voting choice is Party Identification (see above), and the effects of this variable remain fairly constant over our time period.[15]

## Social milieu and issue voting

The apparent inverse relationship between class voting and issue voting may not be quite what it seems. As stated earlier, it is possible that class voting has not declined so much as been replaced by another form of class influence: the influence of social milieu (by which we mean the combined impact of a variety of class factors found in homogenous constituencies). If, as Miller (1978) has suggested, politics has become increasingly about 'people around here' then the apparently increasing effect of issues could simply reflect the dominant issue preferences of 'people around here'.

In order to be able to evaluate this hypothesis, our survey data were supplemented with census data from the 1966 and 1971 census, as described above. Specifically, a single variable measuring the percentage of employers and managers in each constituency within which sampling took place was duplicated in the data for each respondent residing in that constituency. Given the spectacular relationship found by Miller between this variable and constituency election results, it would be surprising if there were no relationship at the individual level between voting choice and constituency class mix. In fact there is such a relationship, with a correlation in the range 0.261 to 0.274 over the period. However, this relationship was at its highest not in 1970 but in 1966, and more importantly changed little with the passage of time. Moreover, the necessary relationship between milieu characteristics and

---

[15] Issue voting, as we have seen, accounted for some 25 per cent of total effects at the start of our period and rose to some 40 per cent by the end. Class voting started by accounting for some 40 per cent of total effects, and declined progressively. Party identification made up the balance of total effects, varying between 35 and 40 per cent over the period. This consistency in the effects of party identification may appear surprising in the light of the well-documented decline in the proportion of strong party identifiers during the same period (see in particular Crewe, Sarlvik, and Alt, 1977). In fact the direct and indirect effects of this variable did decline in our analyses, but so did its connection with social class. So the transmitted effects that have to be deducted in the computation of net influences also declined. Because its declining influence was more and more independent of other influences its net contribution remained largely unchanged.

issue-based party preference was low (in the range of 0.139 to 0.163) and reached its lowest ebb in 1974.[16]

The only clue discernible in the individual-level data as to why the milieu effect should have increased its capacity to predict constituency election results comes in the relationship between social milieu and social class. Within our sample, a certain amount of shuffling of class and constituency residency patterns must have taken place over the period, since a correlation between individual class characteristics and constituency class characteristics which dropped from 0.209 in 1964 to 0.159 in 1966 had, by 1974, risen to 0.308.[17] This change in relationship, suitably magnified in an ecological analysis (see footnote 1), could be the only individual-level concomitant of the constituency-level changes observed by Miller.

At all events the increase in issue-based voting choice, which in our data mirrors the decline in class-based voting choice, seems not to be a spurious concomitant of a rising effect of social milieu. On the contrary, the evidence strongly suggests that the decline of class voting in Britain has permitted a more or less equivalent rise in issue-based voting choice.

### Summary and implications

It would be comforting to be able to conclude that British voting behaviour became more rather than less rational over the decade from 1964 to 1974, as issue voting rose to fill the vacuum left by a decline in the class-structuring of voting choice; but while the evidence we have presented in this chapter is consistent with such a conclusion, it does not lead inevitably to it. We have established conditions necessary for an increase in rational voting behaviour, but not sufficient to prove that there was such an increase.

Our less than definitive findings arise from two deficiencies in our analysis. In the first place, algebraic manipulation of causal paths is not an altogether satisfactory means of resolving problems in recipro-cal causation. We have tried to show that, within a wide margin, any

[16] Various multivariate models were evaluated in case the bivariate pattern of relationships had been biased by other changes in our data, but none of these analyses produced anything other than a reduction of milieu influences on voting choice in 1974.
[17] This change in correlation also reflects a change in the nature of the class index which in 1964 was dominated by occupational characteristics but which by 1974 had become dominated by housing (see Chapter 5).

reasonable degree of reciprocal causation between issue-based party preferences and party identification would yield results comparable to those we have established here. However, we cannot rule out the possibility of a truly pathological combination of relationships producing quite unexpected transmittances for the indirect effects of political attitudes. In the second place, we have not even addressed the question of whether there might be reciprocal causation involved in the relationships between party identification and voting choice, and between political attitudes and voting choice.[18] Any such reciprocity would attenuate the effects of political attitudes which we have measured, though they would be unlikely to change the direction of the trends we established unless they were so strong as to remove completely the effects of issues. This possibility is unlikely, but has not been ruled out in our analysis.

On the other hand, we can be reasonably confident that our measure of issue-based party choice is indeed connected with rationality. This confidence derives both from our verification of correct perceptions in regard to certain issues (footnote 5) and also from the fact that the correlations shown in Table 6.1 indicate widespread agreement by 1983 as to the issues best served by major parties. If the perceptions had no rational basis we would expect the measures of issue-based party choice to be constructed differently for different individuals, as they largely were in 1964 (see Table 6.1), and the issues themselves to correlate not at all with the resulting measures.

Finally, we were concerned as to the comparability of our measures of issue-based party preferences between 1964 and 1983. However, the major change we detect occurred between two elections (1966 and 1970) for which problems of comparability do not arise, and the fit

[18] In American elections, reciprocal causation between voting choice and issue preferences has been found to be very strong, replacing in large part the causal links we have established between party identification and voting in Britain (Page and Jones, 1979, pp. 1083 and 1086). We cannot replicate this analysis in Britain, for reasons given in note 11 above, but careful consideration of the Page and Jones model indicates that had it been simplified to resemble our own, by removing the candidate evaluations variable and consequential causal paths, its implications *regarding issue voting* would have been largely unchanged. Party identification would have appeared to play a larger role, similar to what we find in our British models, but the reciprocal effects on issues would simply have been displaced to this other variable. So we remain confident that our model is adequate for its purpose, which is to allow the extent of issue voting to show itself in reasonable perspective in relation to other effects. The *nature* of these other effects is not central to our argument.

between this finding and the findings presented in Chapter 4 adds plausibility to a supposition that comparability problems have not affected any of the findings reported here.

What we have certainly established in this chapter is that different models of issue voting give rise to different implications for the extent and direction of change in issue voting. The model that we consider most plausible shows issue voting to have increased in step with the decline of class voting. Moreover, the rise in the apparent incidence of issue voting does not appear to be a spurious concomitant of geographic influences on individual behaviour in the shape of Miller's (1978) milieu effect. On the contrary, what evidence we have been able to bring to bear points to the causal primacy of the decline of class voting in opening the way to an increase in the importance of issues in determining the electoral choice of British voters.

These findings have important implications for the future of British politics. For if the decline in the structuring properties of class variables outlined in Chapter 4 had not been accompanied by any increase in the ability of issue-based party preferences to structure partisanship, then the increasingly unsupported edifice of British two-party voting documented in Chapter 5 would have stood at the mercy of whim and chance. But this chapter seems to show that the British electorate has moved to a more sophisticated basis for voting choice. No longer constrained to the same extent by characteristics largely established during childhood, British voters are now more open to rational argument than they were in the past. A party which ignores these developments and relies on past loyalties to bring supporters to the polls is unlikely to be as successful as a party which bases its appeal on careful assessment of the needs and wishes of the voting population, and skilfully presents its policies in terms of issues that are meaningful and salient to them.

# 7
# WHATEVER HAPPENED TO 1970?

The analysis presented in previous chapters has now provided no fewer than four pieces of evidence pointing to 1970 as the year when a new basis for British electoral choice became established. In Chapter 3 we saw how support for the Labour Party declined in that year by ten times the amount we would have expected on the basis of changes in social structure. It was in that election that Labour first lost a large proportion of voters from among social groups which had previously supported the party. The loss of Labour voters from among these groups indeed continued after that date, but at a very much slower rate. In Chapter 4 this insight was fleshed out when we focused upon the loyalty of class members to parties whose support comes mainly from each class. There we saw that after necessary correction had been made for a variety of contaminating influences, this loyalty fell suddenly between 1966 and 1970, remaining roughly constant thereafter. Moreover, the drop was not just in the loyalty of a single class to a particular party. On the contrary, both parties suffered drops of apparently equivalent magnitude in the extent to which they could count on the votes of their natural class supporters. Then in Chapter 5 we looked more deeply at the way in which class underpinned partisanship, and determined that the decline of class voting was associated primarily with a decline in the most central of class influences on voting choice (parents' class and respondent's occupation); a decline which again occurred mainly between 1966 and 1970. Finally, in Chapter 6, we saw that the decline in the structuring effects of social class was matched by an equivalent rise in the effects of issues on voting choice, yet again occurring in the same inter-election period.

Our findings are further confirmed by the independent study of Himmelweite *et al.*, which we discussed in Chapter 2. These researchers also found change to be occurring, and during the same period. They could not say on the basis of their data whether the change was attributable to the ageing of their subjects or to a more general development affecting individuals of different ages. We can now say that the change they detected must have gone beyond the narrow bounds of the single cohort that they studied, or it would not have manifested itself so clearly in the population as a whole. We shall be conducting our own cohort study in a later section of this chapter, but first we must enquire what was special about the 1970 election, at which so many singular changes first manifested themselves.

The election of 1970 was not apparently very remarkable. Its most important feature was a return of the Conservative Party to power, under Edward Heath, after six years of Labour rule under Harold Wilson. On the face of it, this constituted no more than a normal swing of the electoral pendulum between the two dominant parties, with no overt sign of any decay in the class basis upon which choice was made.

The election did show more volatility than had once been customary, with the Tories winning on a last minute swing that was unanticipated by all but one of the commercial opinion polling organizations; and political pundits were much occupied for a time with debates over why the polls had got it wrong. Ultimately it was felt that the unexpected outcome resulted from a combination of two factors of which one indeed was the presence of a late swing to the Conservatives. The other (of more relevance to our current concerns) was a bias in the samples drawn by the polling organizations.

When we look back at Figure 4.7 we see that the major source of new recruits to the Tory ranks in 1970 were individuals from the solidly working-class strata of the population. This flow was to some extent cancelled by a lesser flow to Labour from among solidly middle-class individuals, but it provided the basis for the Tory victory in that year. Now the commercial polling organizations do not employ simple random samples of the British population. They employ stratified or quota samples of a highly clustered nature so as to reduce costs by interviewing a large number of people in a relatively small number of circumscribed areas. This means that it is important for them to be able to anticipate to some extent the normal distribution of opinions over the country in order to be able to correct for any lack of representativeness in the samples they acquire. As long as the basic profile of party support remains unchanged their estimates of changes in national opinion will be quite accurate, but should large changes occur in this profile the clusters may easily fail to reflect these changes. Seen with the advantages of hindsight, it seems likely that this is what happened to the pollsters in 1970.

So the change in the basis of British politics was remarked upon by commentators at the time it occurred. It was not, however, recognized for what it was. Not until 1974, when freedom from traditional party ties first made it possible for large scale defections to occur away from both major parties at the same time, did it become evident that something fundamental had happened to the basis of British politics. At the time it was thought that the rise of minor party voting in 1974 was caused primarily by the attractiveness of the policies of these parties. In retrospect it is clear that the preconditions for change had already been established. With the advantages of hindsight (once again) we can see that it did not take as much for minor parties to do well in 1974 as it would have done ten years previously.

So what did happen, between 1966 and 1970, to open the way to such radical changes? Although other authors may not have been able to point to the period of major change in as unambiguous a way as we have done,[1] other authors have suggested a variety of explanations for the changes that they have detected in British political life. In this chapter we will evaluate some of these explanations in the light of the findings of previous chapters. The explanations fall into two groups: those focusing on social developments as a cause of electoral change, and those focusing on political issues as a cause of electoral change.

### Explanations focusing on social change

We saw in Chapter 3 that many fundamental features of our society have changed in the past twenty years. In particular, this period has seen a transformation of the British educational system, an increase in the proportion of the workforce employed in traditionally middle-class jobs, an enormous increase in union membership (and particularly middle-class union membership), and a decimation of the private rental housing market together with a corresponding rise in the numbers of council tenants and home-owners.

Changes of these kinds can have two sets of consequences. In the first place, as explored in Chapter 3, they can serve to reduce the size of the social groups which used to support the Labour Party and increase the size of the groups which used to support the Conservatives. At the same time, however, the social changes were accompanied by reductions in the power of certain social characteristics to structure partisanship, as we saw in Chapters 4 and 5. These reductions might

[1] Samuel Beer, in his *Britain Against Itself*, indeed points to 1968 as the critical year in which change came to the British electorate (see below).

also be the consequences of social change. For example, a rise in middle-class union membership, unless it led to more middle-class people voting Labour (and so reduced the extent of class voting), would be bound to reduce the relationship between unionization and voting choice. Any increase in the number of children of working-class homes who entered white-collar occupations could lead to a similar trend.

In fact, as we saw in Chapter 5, there was a difference between occupation and union membership in the way in which their effects changed over our time period. The effects of occupation indeed declined dramatically, but those of union membership increased. So the consequences of changing social structure for the effects of class on voting choice are not deducible on a priori grounds. The size and composition of social groups does not translate in simple terms into relationships between group characteristics and voting choice.[2] This means that it will be hard to assess whether changes in social structure have led to the reductions that we have observed in the loyalty to traditional class parties of groups that customarily supported these parties.

Nevertheless, one social change must be treated as a serious candidate for explanatory factor in the events of 1966 to 1970. This is the change that Dunleavy points to (see Chapter 2) from party choice being dominated by occupational characteristics to party choice being dominated by housing. We saw in Chapter 5 that the decline in the power of central class characteristics to structure partisanship was quickly followed by a rise in the power of supportive characteristics to provide a substitute structure largely based on housing and union membership.

Although Dunleavy rejects the basic approach which has led us to our findings, these findings are in fact consistent with Dunleavy's view that party choice has moved from a production cleavage basis to a consumption cleavage basis; and although Dunleavy does not claim this

[2] The strange contrast between increasing effects of union membership when other things are equal (in Chapter 5) and the decreasing relationship between union membership and voting choice when union membership is seen as an isolated factor (in Chapter 3) is resolved if we consider the difference between union membership as a *correlate* of partisanship and union membership as an *effect on* partisanship. Increasing numbers of middle-class union members would serve to reduce the ability of this characteristic to distinguish between Labour supporters and others, and so reduce its correlation with Labour voting. By contrast, the same change increases the opportunity for middle-class individuals to be influenced towards Labour voting by their new experiences as union members. So the effects of union membership could increase even as its value as an indicator declined.

move to have been a cause of all the changes we have seen in recent years, we should consider the possibility that it was. The timing is right: central class variables whose importance declined so dramatically in 1970 are production-oriented, while housing (at any rate) is regarded by Dunleavy as the most important consumption variable.

What does not fit is the underlying rate of social change in the sizes of occupational and housing groups. The tables and illustrations in Chapter 3 showed clearly that the trends were of long standing, and did not show a sudden inflection between 1966 and 1970. So the timing is only right when we consider the changing effects of the characteristics involved. It ceases to be right when we consider the underlying social processes that would have to be fuelling these changing effects. Social changes in the past twenty years have been extensive, and (in comparison with earlier periods in history) no doubt rapid. But they are too slow to account for major changes occurring within a four-year period.

A different type of social change from that which concerned Dunleavy suffers the same problem of insufficient speed, but should still be mentioned in this context. It is possible that technological change can lead to changes in the structure of society, and particularly in the extent to which social groups cohere into mass parties and other concominants of mass society. This notion has been put forward by Alvin Toffler in his *The Third Wave* (1980), where he points out that many features of the post-war world were direct consequences of an industrial revolution which required mass markets, massive workforces, and so forth. These features of social organization resulted from what he saw as the second great wave of change that swept our world (the first was the agricultural revolution). However, according to Toffler (and his thesis is convincingly argued), we are now undergoing a third wave of change, associated with the information-processing revolution, which will make unnecessary the massive social structures upon which our industrial civilization depended.

Mass parties may well have been a product of industrial society, and their breakup into smaller groupings may well result from the more individualistic interests that appear to be a feature of contemporary society. Toffler's description of the consequences of the third wave is certainly consistent with the increasing diversity of political interests that we have documented in past chapters. But the timing is wrong. Not only (as with an emerging consumption cleavage) is the speed of technological change too slow to account for the rapid electoral changes we have observed, but also the electoral changes came too soon to have been the consequences of technological change in British society. By 1970 the potential of the microchip had not even been imagined, and the changes in manufacturing, distribution, and information processing that have dominated our society since the middle 1970s were no more than gleams on a far horizon. Toffler may or may not be right in discerning a 'powerful tide surging across much of the world' (p. 15), but even if he were right in general terms, his anticipated political consequences would only now be being felt. They cannot possibly explain events of twenty years ago.

## Explanations focusing on issue change

The majority of the explanations that have been put forward for the evident recent changes in British politics have focused upon changes in the nature and import of political issues. In a recent volume of *Parliamentary Affairs*, King (1982) points out that changes in parliamentary behaviour since the middle sixties have coincided with the arrival of issues that could not easily be integrated into the pre-existing two-party battle. The same can be said about changes in electoral behaviour. Since the mid-1960s a whole series of issues (generally the same as those King refers to) have become salient which did not fit the existing cleavage between Labour and Conservatives. Just as politicians within each party could not agree with each other to oppose politicians of the other party, so voters could no longer choose their parties by simply picking the one that stood for their preferred issue positions. Conflict within each party over such questions as immigration, common market membership, and devolution for Scotland and Wales meant that voters may not have been able to readily identify a party associated with their own preferences on these and other issues. Thus some voters with a given position might pick one major party, others another major party, and yet a third group might opt for a minor party on the grounds that it offered the best prospect of achieving the same policy objective. Developments of this kind would certainly be consistent with the sort of changes in voting behaviour that we have documented in past chapters, but they hardly constitute an explanation for the changes. In order for this type of analysis to yield a satisfactory explanation, we have to be able to say why new issues arose then and not before, and why the parties were not able to integrate their approach to these issues as they had managed to do in the past.

Moreover, the approach is unsatisfactory for another reason as well.

We have established (particularly in Chapter 6) that until 1970 issues were not particularly important in determining voting choice. So not only do we need to explain why issues arose that were not properly integrated into the party system, but also why the electorate started to concern itself with such issues in the first place.

We will put this second question to one side for the moment, and focus on the prior question of why issues arose which were different from those that the party system had previously articulated so well. One possible reason takes us back to social change. For though social change might not be rapid enough on its own to bring about changes in voting behaviour of the magnitude of those observed between 1966 and 1970, it might nevertheless act as a trigger to bring about changes in attitudes. It is a well established fact (central to the argument of previous chapters) that people react to the opinions of those around them, generally in such a way as to conform to an opinion or attitude that is perceived as dominant. But what gives to an attitude its dominant stature? If the attitude is linked to the posession of some social attribute (ownership or otherwise of one's home, for example) then the more people who own their own homes, the more likely is an attitude associated with this attribute to be perceived as dominant. Indeed, one can imagine a mechanism in which a very small amount of social change could result in a very large extent of issue change just because the number of people with some issue-linked attribute had risen above a critical threshold.

On the basis of an argument such as this, a consumption cleavage theorist might propose that Dunleavy had been right in pointing to the new primacy of a housing cleavage in structuring voting choice since 1970, simply because the number of individuals with clear personal interests affected by this cleavage had risen. People with certain attitudes resulting from their housing situation could suddenly have become dominant within their social circles, and the importance of housing as an issue would therefore have suddenly increased.

A major problem with such an argument is that housing did not suddenly become a salient issue in 1970. It has indeed slowly become an issue dividing the parties in the years since then, but even today it is not, as we saw in Chapter 2, an issue of sufficient importance as to permit us to identify it as the basis of voting choice.

So it does not appear reasonable to assert that the rise of issue voting can give back to social changes (through the back door, as it were) an importance that direct analysis of their consequnces appears to deny them.

This does not mean that social change has no part to play in bringing about the developments we have detected in recent British voting behaviour. What it means is that social changes cannot be credited with influences beyond those that we can directly measure. We have already seen that about half of the decline in the extent of Labour voting since 1970 can be credited to social change, and we will see later in this chapter that social changes other than those we have already analysed have had consequences as well. Nevertheless, there is still space for issue change to have had an effect in its own right in changing the nature of British political life, and we will now turn to some accounts of issue change that purport to explain recent developments in voting behaviour.

Most of these explanations can be dismissed straight away because they focus on issue changes that clearly occurred later than 1970, but two books point to developments in the late 1960s that could account for the events of 1970, at least in part. The first of these to be published was Samual Beer's *Britain Against Itself* (1982) and the second was Paul Whiteley's *The Labour Party in Crisis* (1983) which we have already discussed in Chapter 2. However, we will deal with them in reverse order of publication, looking at Whiteley's analysis first.

### Reactions to policy failures

Whiteley's thesis is directed only at explaining the decline in Labour party support, rather than at explaining the decline in class-based support for both parties. However, to the extent that the thesis succeeds in explaining one phenomenon, it will contribute to an explanation of the other since working-class defectors from the Labour party (unless they abstain from voting) have to put their crosses somewhere on the ballot paper, and if they end up voting for Conservative candidates they will contribute to the decline of class voting.

Whiteley's argument is very simple: Labour lost support because it failed to implement the policies it promised. In particular, Whiteley claims that in 1964 and 1966 it promised economic growth and improvements in the circumstances of poor people, and failed to deliver either of these sets of benefits by 1970. Defections of erstwhile Labour supporters in 1970 can thus be seen as resulting from unfavourable evaluations of Labour performance in government. Whiteley tries to show that, at least in 1979, what he refers to as 'retrospective evaluations' of past successes and failures by the Labour party were powerful determinants of voting choice, and he strongly implies that the same would have been true in 1970.

But Whiteley's thesis has a flaw when it comes to applying it (which he never explicitly does) to the events of 1970. Retrospective voting requires awareness of current affairs and an ability to apportion credit and blame for policy successes and failures. It is a sophisticated activity which Whiteley distinguishes from the less specific feelings of approval and disapproval that he refers to as 'affective evaluations'. Individuals who are capable of retrospective evaluations are likely to be better educated than those who base their voting choice on a more straight-forward view of how much they 'liked' each party (Whiteley, 1983, p. 95). Yet when we consider the kind of people who actually reacted against the Labour government of 1966–70, these are, in fact, the least well educated voters. Figure 4.7 showed quite clearly that the largest swings away from Labour voting occurred in the solidly working-class strata: those with at least five of the six working-class attributes associated with working-class origins, including a minimal education. Whiteley's figures show that only about a quarter of the effects on voting choice result from retrospective concerns,[3] so it is surely not likely that these effects should be associated with the voters of least sophistication.

On the other hand, the prevalence of retrospective evaluations might be more widespread than Whiteley's figures show. He does not take account of the indirect effects which we saw in Chapter 6 to have such an important part to play in assessing the extent of issue

[3] Whiteley does not prove, even for the 1979 data that he analyses, that evaluations of past performance dominate electoral choice. On the contrary, his own findings (Table 4.3 and the relevant text) show clearly that affective evaluations are the most powerful. Retrospective evaluations are indeed more important than evaluations of likely future performance (by a margin of 0.27 to 0.21 when the effects of each group of predictors in his Table 4.3 are summed), but they are much less important than affective evaluations (0.38) and account for only about a quarter of the total effects displayed in the table. If the same pattern were to have held true in 1970, loss of working-class support for the Labour party in that year would likely have been due to people defecting for reasons other than policy failures, in a ratio of three to one. Of course the same pattern might not hold true in 1970, but our findings in this book show that to have been the year in which issue voting first took the form that has continued since that time.

voting.[4] If Whiteley's analysis were to take these into account, then it is possible that it would show retrospective voting to be sufficiently important to account for a quite large part of the events of 1970. We will return to this suggestion in a later section.

## Collectivist contradictions

One of the few political analysts to actually point to the election of 1970 as being the first of a new era is Samuel Beer, who in fact picks out 1968 as the year in which that era dawned. In *Britain Against Itself* Beer suggests that the consensus that had been bred within British parties by the successes of post-war collectivism (by which term he means 'that thrust of policy, emerging in this century, toward control over the economic and social order as a whole') started to break down in Britain during the middle 1960s, as symbolized (according to Beer) by the student revolts of 1968. The reasons for the breakdown he ascribes to contradictions within the collectivist system which led to a pay scramble, benefits scramble, and subsidy scramble that could not be sustained indefinitely. Beer sees the declining importance of class as linked to these developments, and providing a precondition for what he calls 'the new populism'. The latter term is used to cover the emergence of new issues that do not fit well within the two-party structure that existed in 1970.

What Beer has done is twofold. Firstly, he has characterized the developments in voting behaviour that we have been concerned with in this book, and developed an account of these developments that relates them to each other and to other strands in the British political

---

[4] Whiteley's regression analysis finds no place for the variable which in our (Chapter 6) analyses showed itself paramount in determining voting choice: party identification. Indeed, it seems likely that Whiteley's 'affective' variable (respondent's liking of the Labour party) might actually be a party identification variable under another guise. But we also know from Chapter 6 that party identification is partially consequential upon issues, and if retrospective issues are the most important of those left when affective orientation is redefined into a measure of party identification, then retrospective issues are going to be having important indirect effects on voting choice by way of their effects on party identification. So they will have been relatively more important than Whiteley's analysis shows. Moreover, we also know from earlier chapters that party identification is not independent of social attributes, so that in a causal analysis where social attributes are given credit for their indirect effects, the net effects of affective evaluations will be less than those that Whiteley finds. So, *in relation to* other bases of voting choice, retrospective evaluations will gain a second boost from such a redefinition of the framework of analysis.

tradition. From this point of view his approach complements our own by putting flesh on the bones we have so painstakingly dissected. Secondly, he has provided an explanation for the developments, and in this his contribution is less helpful. For in pointing to processes that could not continue indefinitely (the three scrambles), Beer does not show why they terminated when they did, nor why their termination was associated with the particular changes in voting behaviour that in fact occurred.

However, Beer's approach does have one feature of great potential importance in showing us a way forward. His 'new populism' is associated with a change in political viewpoint that he assumes to have been particularly prevalent among young voters, and he quotes Inglehart in support of this assumption.

## A silent revolution?

In an article published in the *American Political Science Review*, which forms the basis for a later book, Ronald Inglehart (1971, 1977) proposed that a transformation might well have been taking place in the political cultures of advanced industrial societies: a transformation which affected the stand taken on current political issues by large sections of the electorate, and which might have been expected to have a long-term tendency to alter existing patterns of political partisanship.[5] This transformation, Inglehart felt, arose from the emergence on the political scene of a new middle-class group (sons and daughters of middle-class parents) who, far from feeling the need to increase their security or advance their status through the aquisition of material posessions, had been socialized during a long period of unprecedentedly high affluence, so that they were able to take economic security for granted. Among members of this new group a set of 'post-bourgeois' values, relating to the need for belonging and to aesthetic and intellectual needs, seemed to have taken the place of the more 'aquisitive' values of those who had experienced the wars and scarcities which preceeded the West European economic miracles (Inglehart, 1971, p. 991).

Initial testing of this hypothesis in Britain indicated that, while it

[5] Much of the material presented in this section is derived from a paper which I wrote in collaboration with Ronald Inglehart, and presented to a meeting of the British Political Studies Association in 1973. I am grateful to my co-author for allowing me to make use of the fruits of our joint research in this book.

was indeed possible to differentiate between aquisitive and post-bourgeois sections of the electorate, the emergence of the new middle-class group had as yet had remarkably little impact upon the balance of party support in this country (pp. 1015-16). So the changes we detected in that year cannot, on the basis of Inglehart's findings, be straightforwardly ascribed to the silent revolution.

Several reasons might be put forward to account for this apparent lack of impact, but two are particularly relevant to our present discussion. In the first place, whatever may have been the situation in other countries, in Britain the emergence of a post-bourgeois group with the attitudes hypothesized would be less than revolutionary. For a stress on aesthetic and intellectual needs is not new in Britain. Such individualistic values have always constituted an important strand in British élite opinion, despite the espousal by both major parties of collectivist values in the years following 1945 (cf. Beer, 1965). So the fact that a post-bourgeois section of the electorate could be detected does not indicate that the same attitudes were not present in previous elections.

In the second place, it might well be argued that the small impact of the transformation was due to the relative rigidity of a long-established two-party system. At an election in which meaningful change could only come from individuals switching their votes from one major party to another, it is perhaps to be expected that a transformation of the kind we hypothesize should have had relatively less impact upon the political system than in countries where a greater number of effective parties permit political allegiances to change in smaller gradations. In continental European countries the distribution of the electorate between aquisitive and post-bourgeois categories was found to relate markedly to party preference (Inglehart, 1971, p. 1010).

In our paper for the Political Studies Association (Franklin and Inglehart, 1973), we employed Smallest Space Analysis to try and picture the attitude space of the British electorate in 1970, in order to see how attitudes associated by Inglehart with the post-bourgeois phenomenon were related to more traditional attitudes and to preferences for political parties and personalities. The results may be thought of as a map or chart, in which attitudes held in common by the same individuals are pictured in proximity to one another, while attitudes which do not go together are pictured at some distance apart.

The data for this study came from a Louis Harris poll which had been especially commissioned by Inglehart for his European project, and the Smallest Space Analysis reproduced in Figure 7.1 does show what might be termed a 'new left' quadrant in which attitudes associated with post-bourgeois values are indeed distinguished from more traditional left-wing concerns. The illustration is reproduced as it came from the computer, with left-wing attitudes depicted towards the right of the chart. The analysis was constrained to produce a two-dimensional solution because this is all that can be depicted on a flat sheet of paper, and because our interests focused on whether two dimensions would distinguish post-bourgeois from other values.

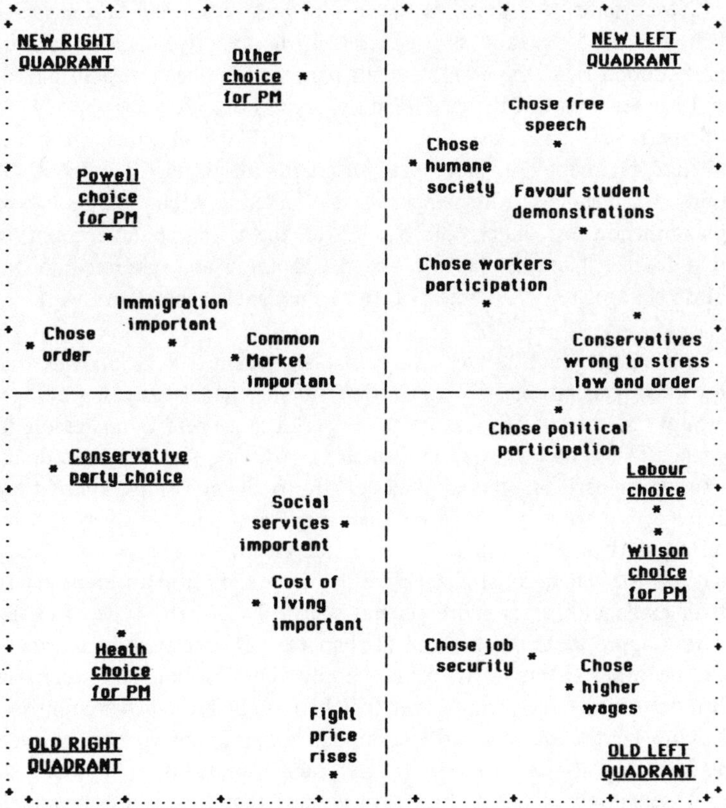

Figure 7.1.    Smallest space configuration of attitude, party choice,
and Prime Ministerial preference variables among
all respondents, 1970.

*Source:* Reproduced from Franklin and Inglehart (1973).

Unfortunately, none of the post-election studies analysed in previous chapters contain precisely this set of variables. When attitudes measured in 1974 and 1979 are subjected to the same type of analysis, again constrained to a two-dimensional solution, a recognizably similar space emerges; but the election studies conducted in 1970 and before simply did not ask the sort of questions that would permit us to monitor the evolution of the issue space. Thus we cannot tell whether the election of 1970 marked a turning point in the attitude structure of British voters, or whether the same pattern would have been found in 1964 and 1966.

Nevertheless, it is possible that a silent revolution did take place in Britain after 1966, and showed itself in the underlying social basis of party support. At this level it might perhaps have been responsible for at least some part of the decline in the loyalty of middle-class groups to the party of their class that occurred in 1970 and which we documented in Chapter 4. Moreover, Inglehart's insight (1971, pp. 992-3) that working-class voters may have reacted to the post-bourgeois phenomenon by undergoing a shift to the right, could account in part for the fact that (as we saw in Chapter 4 and reiterated above) most change in 1970 came not from middle-class but from working-class groups.

Above all, Inglehart's insight that the silent revolution was one involving generational change, rather than a change affecting all age-groups, is one that should be taken seriously. There is no reason to suppose that the changes in British class voting that we have documented in past chapters applied equally to all age-groups, and if they applied primarily to new voters then they would manifestly have been different than if they had applied to the electorate as a whole. Explanations for generational change are to be looked for in different places than explanations for more general social change: the type of explanation appropriate to one kind of change is not necessarily appropriate to the other. Even if we cannot apply the post-bourgeois thesis in Britain in quite the manner that Inglehart applied it in other countries, it will nevertheless be of critical importance to know whether we need a thesis that applies primarily to the young or not. For this we need to look separately at the different age cohorts that constitute the British electorate.

The chances of attributing electoral change to those who entered the electorate in 1970 are unusually good, because the size of the group of new voters in 1970 was unusually great. Not only was this the year in which the children of the post-war 'baby boom' first reached voting age, but it was also the year in which the voting age was first reduced from 21 to 18. So a large number of people voted in 1970 who would not otherwise have voted until 1974 thus swelling (on a once-only basis) the size of the incoming electorate.

## Cohort analysing political change

In Chapter 1 we saw that an electoral cohort is generally thought of as constituting those voters who enter the electorate at the time of a particular election, and when we look separately at the abnormally large cohort which voted for the first time in 1970, we do see differences between it and earlier cohorts; but the differences are not marked. Young voters are always expected to be more liable to political change than their elders who have had more time to become innoculated by repeated reaffirmation of earlier political choices (Butler and Stokes, 1974, p. 60), and so we would always expect a swing between parties to result primarily from the movements of young voters. What we need to know in order to be able to assess the possibility that young voters were responsible for the drop in class voting between 1966 and 1970, is how different electoral cohorts reflected their class characteristics in their 1970 voting behaviour, and whether this reflection was different from that seen in earlier years.

To perform this analysis we have calculated for each voter in each election year between 1964 and 1979 a residual which reflects the difference between his or her actual vote and the vote that would have been expected on the basis of class characteristics. The expected vote for each year was calculated from the regression analyses reported in Chapters 1 and 5, so the residuals reflect precisely the lack of loyalty of each class group to the party of the appropriate class. But if the analyses focus on the prediction of Labour voting choice, residuals among Labour voters will get smaller as class responsiveness diminishes, at the same time as residuals among Conservative voters increase. Because of this, analyses of the pattern of class voting residuals among different cohorts at different elections has to be performed separately for each party. Figure 7.2 reports the result of such an analysis for Labour-voting respondents.

In this illustration three groups of voters are distinguished in each of the election years studied. The first group consist of those old enough to have had an opportunity to vote in the election of 1924.

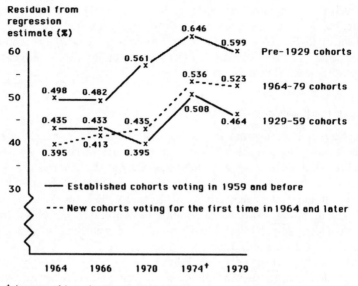

Figure 7.2.   Average residual from perfect class voting among
Labour supporters, from regression analysis of all respondents
by age cohorts, 1964–79 (See Chapter 5 for details)

The second group consists of those voters who entered the electorate
between 1929 and 1959. The third group consists of those voters who
entered the electorate in 1964 or later. As the years depicted in Figure
7.2 go by, so the first group becomes smaller and the third group larger,
as people die and are replaced by new voters. And at each election, the
average age of those contained in each cohort increases. Thus in 1964,
some members of the pre-1929 cohort could have been as young as 61
years old, while by 1983 the youngest remaining member of this group
would have been over 80.

The choice of these three particular groups was made on the basis of
inspecting each election cohort separately. I had hoped to be able to
divide the cohorts in our samples into two groups: those who entered
the electorate in 1970 or later, and those who entered the electorate
before 1970. This was not found to be possible since the largest residual
differences between expected and actual voting were found among
those who entered the electorate in 1924 or before, and a distinctive
group of young voters was found to have existed ever since 1964.

iffered from those who entered the electorate in previous
many of them had not done two years in Her Majesty's
as National Servicemen. Compulsory military service was
abolished between 1958 and 1960, and by 1962 there
year-olds who had been subjected to this experience.

nction of the abolition of conscription and the entry into
e of a distinctive political cohort could be coincidental.
1 shows that National Servicemen in 1964 (the only year
characteristic has been measured) all showed a distinctive
be more influenced by class factors, in contrast to voters
ver in the army, or those who fought in world wars or
gulars.

tely, since we do not know which of the 1970 voters were
vicemen, we cannot discover whether older voters who
have escaped conscription were like the younger voters in
ur that year. And even if we could conduct this test, and
tional Service effect operating in that election, this would
a contention that abolition of National Service is the
ve been looking for. When some people escape an experi-
quite general, the consequences for them are likely to
from what happens when the experience is abolished
hus the women in our samples do not differ in their 1970
iour from men of the same ages, and women did not
pulsory military service. Yet the attitudes of the women

*Average residuals from perfect class voting among Labour
servative respondents by type of military service, from
regression analysis of all respondents, 1964\**

| ary service | Labour | | Conservative | |
|---|---|---|---|---|
| | N | Residual | N | Residual |
| ever served | 449 | 0.457 | 386 | 0.493 |
| rvice | 123 | 0.453 | 85 | 0.491 |
| , etc. | 13 | 0.474 | 20 | 0.397 |
| iceman | 34 | 0.379 | 28 | 0.391 |
| | 619 | 0.453 | 519 | 0.484 |

n analysis for Labour voting is described in Chapter 5.
s procedure was undertaken for measuring class effects on Con-
g in order to derive the Conservative residual employed in this

Surprisingly, after all that has been established about the importance
of the election of 1970, the cohort that entered the electorate in that
year turns out not to have been distinctive. It simply joined a group of
cohorts that had existed for six years already and which was further
enlarged in later elections.

The distinctiveness of the pre-1929 cohorts is easy enough to explain
in retrospect. Between the elections of 1924 and 1929 the Labour vote
increased by over 50 per cent from just under five and a half million
to nearly 8.4 million (Craig, 1968, pp. 6-7). Also, the election of 1929
was the first at which Labour had more Members of Parliament elected
(287) than any other party. So the cohort that entered the electorate in
1929 (swollen by newly-enfranchised women under 30) will have been
socialized during the years of Labour's rise to major party status, and
first had the chance to express a political preference in the election that
saw this status confirmed (at the previous election Labour had won
only 151 seats). It is not surprising that they and their successors
provided the core of the class-based vote for that party.

What is more unexpected is to discover that the cohorts of 1964 and
later were also distinctive. They were distinctive at the elections of
1964 and 1966 in being *more* responsive to the party of their class
(having a *lower* residual in Figure 7.2) than earlier cohorts; and they
were distinctive in the election of 1970 in joining the new voters of that
year in being *less* responsive to Labour party appeals than the 1929-
1959 cohorts (the pre-1929 cohorts remain the least responsive
throughout). Indeed, the most dramatic feature of Figure 7.2 is the way
in which it shows the residual for the youngest cohorts changing places
with that for the next older group in 1970. These younger cohorts
then remain *less* loyal to Labour at every election thereafter. Residuals
for each group of cohorts increase in 1974 and fall back again in 1979,
in step with changes in minor party voting in those elections; but the
three groups of cohorts move roughly in parallel during those years,
as they did before 1970. Analysis of Conservative voters (not shown)
yields essentially the same pattern of findings.

It should be mentioned that Figure 7.2 also shows a distinctive
pattern on the part of the cohorts of 1929-1959, who became *more*
responsive to Labour party appeals in 1970, against the general trend
of that year. It is really change on the part of both groups of cohorts,
rather than change on the part of young voters alone, that gives rise
to the apparently dramatic crossing over of these two groups. However,
we saw in Chapter 4 that class voting can vary for all sorts of reasons,

so that changes from election to election can only really be assessed in relative terms. The 1929-1959 group of cohorts constitutes by far the largest portion of the electorate in 1970, and so serves as the basis for any comparisons. Seen in this light, what Figure 7.2 shows is that, but for the relative decline in class voting on the part of young voters in 1970, Labour would have won the election in that year. Class voting also declined among the oldest voters in our samples, but this will have been more than counterbalanced by the rise in class loyalty among the largest group of cohorts.

Whatever it was that happened in 1970, it thus had its greatest effect on the young (those under 28 in 1970) and on the old (those over 66). These were the groups who had been least effectively socialized into the existing two-party system: those who had entered the electorate before Labour became a major party, and those too young to have had a chance to cast a vote in more than one or two elections.

### A swinging sixties effect?

But for the participation of the pre-1929 cohorts in the events of 1970, it would be tempting to conclude that those events were the outcome of effects initially felt only by the young. But perhaps too much should not be made of the decline of class voting among older cohorts in 1970. Their distinctiveness appears to have been at its greatest in that election and to have declined thereafter (presumably as a result of death among the very oldest individuals in these cohorts), whereas the relative position taken up in that year by younger cohorts is maintained in subsequent elections. Indeed the distinctiveness of younger cohorts in comparison to the 1929-59 cohorts is accentuated in 1979. So whatever caused the oldest cohorts to change their behaviour in 1970 might have been transitory, and unrelated to the effects on young voters which were more permanent.

This line of argument leads us to look for effects that might have influenced young voters during the decade of the 1960s, and such effects are not hard to find. These were, after all, the years during which a 'youth culture' was first established — with long hair, blue jeans, mini skirts, and the Beatles distinguishing those born after 1942 from all those born before. It would be unsurprising to discover that this generation also differed from previous electoral cohorts in their political concerns. In particular, the youth culture was a classless (or perhaps more precisely a cross-class) phenomenon, with youngsters

from different social background distinguish from one-another on t time activities (Marwick, 1982, p. assume that the political concerns class-bound as well.

The trouble with this hypothe such changes to take political eff electoral cohort being rather less chance of a more extended period before first having the opportunit different from the 1970 cohort in to compare their behaviour). Mor of individuals who first reached t year moving back from 1964 tow typical of voters who entered th found among voters entering the behaviour is less obvious in 19 indistinguishable from those wh talking about small groups of ind made of this observation. It *coul* (individual years do sometimes s and 1962 are the first years in that was not visible before and c date may be in doubt, but it mu too early for the Beatles or any yet had a noticeable impact.

### The National Service phenomeno

Our investigations in this book We started with a desire to expl detective work led us to 1970 became evident. Now we hav distinctively in 1970 are those year, and also those who first year back to 1961. So what ha happened, but one feature of t

[6] This analysis was only possib in order to obtain enough examples

year wh
years is
armed f
progress
were few

The
the elec
But Tab
in which
tendency
who wer
among th

Unfor
National
happened
their beh
found no
not disp
trigger w
ence that
be differ
altogether
voting be
undergo

Table 7.
*and (*

Type of m

Female an
World War
Regular ar
National S

Totals

* The regres
An analog
servative vo
chapter.

may be expected to have been influenced by the attitudes of the men with whom they were most closely associated, so this observation does not invalidate the possibility of a National Service effect.

So we are still left with speculation supported only by hints of evidence. The abolition of National Service, of course, had profound effects on British society. For the first time it became possible for young people to make some money before getting married, and this provided fuel for the youth culture that emerged soon afterwards. And it changed the basic orientation towards life of many young men, and the women they married. Life became less serious when the army ceased to play a part in it.

Nor is it hard to imagine why the National Service experience (while it existed) could have served to strengthen class consciousness. For many individuals it will have been their first contact with members of another class, distinguished clearly by being officers or men. Although many 'men' will have had middle-class origins, there were almost no working-class officers. And, in the army, men take orders from officers, so a certain class stereotype is reinforced. Table 7.1 does not show the effects to have been very great, but even an effect of small magnitude has importance if it can suddenly be removed. This one was, by government decree.

## Why 1970?

Clearly the National Service effect is not enough, by itself, to explain the events of 1970 and later; but if we put together all the evidence we have amassed in this and previous chapters, we can reach some tentative conclusions about the nature of the change that the British electorate underwent during the 1960s.

At the start of that decade British voting behaviour was characterized by the existence of two age-cohorts among the voters: those socialized before the emergence of Labour to major party status, and those socialized after that time. The latter group displayed class-conscious voting that has continued to the present day, while the former group has always been much less influenced by class-related concerns. By the end of the decade a third age-cohort had emerged, more class conscious than the pre-1929 cohorts, but increasingly less constrained by class than those socialized during the intervening thirty years.

Why this new group of voters should have been disposed towards behaving distinctively cannot be definitively established, but theory and evidence both point to the importance of increasing affluence which had its greatest effect on young voters for whom the abolition of National Service provided a turning-point after which the affluence was felt quite suddenly. The abolition of National Service will also have removed a particular reinforcement to class consciousness; and class consciousness will surely have been further eroded by the un-classbound youth culture which then grew up.

The most remarkable feature of the new group of voters who emerged from 1961 onwards lies in the fact that its distinctiveness remained no more than potential until the election of 1970. What it was that caused it to distinguish itself in that election and not before is something that all our investigations have failed to uncover. What follows is only a suggestion that I can think of no means for substantiating, but a strong hypothesis would link the change to efforts by the Labour party leadership to make of that party a 'natural party of government'. This was indeed an objective explicitly espoused by Harold Wilson from 1964 onwards (Butler and Pinto-Duschinsky, 1971, pp. 1–6).

The Parliament elected in 1966 provided the first Labour majority in fifteen years that was large enough to have a chance to build upon the achievements of 1945–1950. The Parliament of 1966 thus provided the first opportunity for young Labour voters to become disillusioned with the prospects for a socialist Britain. The same election will also have provided the first opportunity in fifteen years for the party to prove to potential supporters from middle-class backgrounds that it was content to govern a mixed society. This latter objective was the one Harold Wilson espoused. Paradoxically, his very success in achieving this objective may have been what cost the party so much support among members of the working class. Young voters may have ceased to see any great class difference between the parties during this period, and so become responsive to appeals that were not class based. This hypothesis is no more than speculative, but it does fit the facts that we have so painstakingly uncovered.

If this hypothesis is indeed correct (and I repeat that I can see no way of proving it so) then retrospective voting of a kind will have taken place: a possibility that we left open earlier in this chapter. But if this was retrospective voting, it was not of the sort envisaged by Whiteley (see above). The sorts of policy failures that Whiteley associated with this type of voting were those that would have been felt mainly by established Labour voters. But we have found that established Labour voters were not those who deserted the party in 1970. Quite the contrary. It was the tentative and the sometime Labour voters who deserted, heralding in the process a post-collectivist era.

## The post-collectivist era

The nature of this era is by now familiar to us. It is one filled with new and unexpected political developments. In the mid-1970s nationalism in Scotland became a powerful political force, rising suddenly to prominence and declining again just as rapidly. In 1981 the Social Democrats were formed, and for a time their alliance with the Liberal party appeared unstoppable as by-election after by-election gave them additional Parliamentary seats. Even at the time of writing (early 1984) an Alliance breakthrough cannot be written off, with the two smaller parties replacing either Labour or Conservative as a major party at the next election. The analysis presented in this book does not tell us whether such a change in political alignment will come about. What can be said is that the opportunity for realignment is there, and has been there since 1970.

The SDP/Liberal alliance may well fail to push over the spineless structure which in 1983 still supported the old two-party system, and no other new force may prove capable of doing so. Nevertheless, so long as class voting does not reassert itself, and no other change gives an alternative source of stability to electoral choice, each new political force will have the *potential* for breaking through. So we can expect the volatility in electoral preferences that has marked the politics of recent years to continue, and minor parties to gain and lose electoral support with changes in political fashion. One or more of these small parties may indeed attain major party status in favourable circumstances, but in their turn such parties will then be vulnerable to the same fickleness in electoral choice that was responsible for their rise. So as long as the social bases of political choice remain as I have described them, elections in Britain appear unlikely to regain the predictability they enjoyed until the elections of 1974. This in turn may encourage politicians to bid for electoral support with policies and promises that might not otherwise have been voiced, and electoral reactions to these bids for support could add still more to the uncertainty surrounding electoral outcomes.

So the era we have entered as a result of the decline of class voting is not characterized by a realignment of the party system. Realignment implies permanence, and a new party in as secure an electoral position as were the major parties of old. The present social bases of voting choice do not give such security of tenure to any party, new or old (see Chapter 5). In fact the only change that is likely to result immediately from the decline of class voting has already come about. The decline has led to an era of uncertainty in electoral outcomes unparalleled in fifty years. This uncertainty could in turn lead to realignment, with the social bases of party choice solidifying around a new party system which, instead of being class-based, might be based on regional, employment, or even consumption cleavages. But such a development must take time to evolve, and there is little hint as yet of what direction it might take. For the indefinite future we can expect to continue living in interesting political times.

## Summary and assessment

In this book we have established four propositions of major importance:
(1) About half of the decline in support for the Labour party that occurred between 1966 and 1979 can be attributed to changes in social structure which had the effect of reducing the size of class groups that had provided the bulk of Labour votes in 1964.
(2) The rest of the decline that took place up to 1979 (and probably most of the further decline that was evident in 1983) is attributable to the reduced appeal of Labour to the groups that had traditionally supported it. A similar decline in Conservative support among traditionally Tory social groups made this a quite general phenomenon of declining class voting.
(3) The decline in the class basis of voting amounts to a weakening of constraints on volatility and self-expression and the consequence was to open the way to choice between parties on the basis of issue preferences. This is reflected both in the rise of new parties to respond to new issue concerns, and also in a change in the basis for choice between pre-existing parties. Above all it has led to the uncertainty in electoral outcomes which is a primary characteristic of contemporary politics.
(4) All these developments have their origins in events that occurred before 1970, which is the first election to clearly show the new bais for party choice. The events had most effect on younger voting cohorts: those who had entered the electorate after 1959.

These propositions have been established with great care, on the basis of analysis grounded on previously well-substantiated findings. The four propositions are thus not open to serious challenge unless the data upon which they are based prove faulty or our methods of analysis can be improved upon.[7]

What we have not been able to do with equal authority is to establish the reason or reasons for the changes that occurred. Though we have managed to employ our empirical findings in order to cast doubt on the explanations given by other authors, our own explanation survives not because it has passed some equivalent empirical test but only because it was not possible to define one.

It is of course a fundamental tenet of the scientific method that a proposition that is not falsifiable has no status in truth. However, our proposition does not strictly come into this category. It might be falsifiable in principle, but not with the means we have to hand. To recapitulate, what we have proposed is essentially that class voting declined when it became clear that the major restructuring of society Labour had promised to inaugurate in 1945 was complete. A Labour government under Wilson could be seen by its more ideological supporters (I do not wish to imply that most of Labour's 1966 supporters voted for socialism), as well as by those who might have feared such developments, to have taken no further steps towards the establishment of a Socialist Britain. Instead Labour appeared to have become a party whose purpose was to win office, for no better reason than to hold the reins of power. Its programme had become to influence in minor ways the administration of a society whose essential character was no longer in question. Shorn of its ideological commitments, Labour became a party of government, to be evaluated at election time

---

[7] In particular it is possible that an alternative data source would yield findings that differed in detail from those we have established. This is because many of these details must be subject to sampling error, and another sample would certainly incorporate different errors. At the time of writing a project is under way at the University of Strathclyde, supported by a grant from the ESRC, to validate some of the variables we have employed in this book by comparing them with data collected by the Conservative party in private polls. Our methods of analysis are also open to improvement. The major need is to be able to disentangle the reciprocal causation we established in Chapter 6, between party identification and issues. If we could establish what sort of people in what circumstances were affected by which issues to change their party allegiance, this would greatly increase our understanding of the preconditions for electoral change. Unfortunately, no one has yet elaborated a methodology for handling the problem.

(particularly by younger voters) in terms of whether it could offer more effective and attractive policies than its major opponent. Once both major parties came to be evaluated in this way, class would have much less to do with voting choice than had been the case when Labour's appeal was more largely to class interest and solidarity. Moreover, this style of government required policies to be introduced that would not necessarily please all those who had voted Labour. This means that the way was open for electoral change, with opportunities for post-bourgeois and other value systems to play a part, and even for retro-spective assessments among some groups of voters.

The hypothesis is straightforward, appealing, and fits the facts we have uncovered; but at best it is probably no more than part of the truth. If there is any single theme running through the pages of this book, it is that social life is infinitely complex, and simple explanations are unable to do it justice. So while a Labour party running out of steam may provide a reason why some voters shook themselves free of class ties in 1970, it is doubtful whether it constitutes a full expla-nation. Certainly we thought we established in Chapter 6 that the decline of class voting opened the way to a rise in issue voting, but our analysis there did not rule out the possibility that while class voting stood in the way of issue voting for most people, for some it may have been the other way around. And if we allow the possibility that issues arose that weaned voters away from old allegiances, then the number of possible explanations for change in 1970 become virtually limitless. This is especially true when we bear in mind that the issues involved were idiosyncratic to particular voters, without any overriding concern that caught the attention of large numbers of people.[8]

So it seems to me important that we leave open the possibility of multiple explanations for changes in British voting choice. This is especially true when we consider that Britain is not the only country that has seen changes of a similar type in recent years. In the United States and in the Netherlands books have been published that docu-ment changes in the nature of electoral choice which look astonishingly like the changes that have occurred in Britain (Verba, Nie, and Petrocik,

---

[8]  Recent research in the United States (Tuckel and Tejera, 1983) suggests that the major characteristic of recent elections in that country is what these authors call the 'particularization' of voting choice, with different voters reacting to different particular concerns; and analysis of the particular issues of major concern in recent British elections shows a similar distribution. This was shown for 1979 in Figure 2.3, but is evident also in our data for 1970.

1981; Van der Eijk and Neimoller, 1983). But these authors explain the changes in ways that are quite different from the explanation we have given (and quite different from the explanations given by each other). So it behoves us to be cautious in accounting for British electoral change by means of explanations which are unique to Britain, and could not apply elsewhere.

Nevertheless, the explanation we have given for the events of the 1960s should retain its importance even in the context of a more developed view of the mainsprings of political change. Moreover, it appears unlikely to be supplanted on the basis of re-analysis of existing data. To advance further we need a new perspective, and one promising avenue would be a comparative study of electoral change in several political systems. From such a study we might derive new insights that would permit us to elaborate and extend the view of electoral change that has been developed in this book.

# APPENDIX

In this appendix we review some features of our data. For the most part these derive from post-election surveys conducted at Oxford University or the University of Essex. Documentation on the Oxford surveys of 1963, 1964, 1966, and 1970 is to be found in Butler and Stokes (1974). Documentation on the Essex surveys of 1974 and 1979 is to be found in Sarlvik and Crewe (1983). The 1983 Gallup survey employed principally in Chapter 6 is poorly documented, and the findings we report have to be treated with caution for this reason as well as for reasons given in the text.

The use of most variables contained in these surveys is straightforward, as described in Chapter 3. However, in the case of the six standard social structural variables employed throughout this study, it is important to note that missing data was not always excluded. Because of differences in coding and question format from survey to survey, the only way to achieve comparability was sometimes to include 'DK, NA' answers along with those who *did not have* the attribute of interest. Thus parents' party was assumed to be non-Labour if no information was available about parents' party preference. Other social structural variables treated in this way were years of education and occupational grade.

When these are used in order to explain why some respondents should support one major party while other respondents support the other major party, each of our six social structure variables had to be dichotomized in such a way as to group together characteristics associated with Labour party voting, and distinguish these from characteristics associated with Conservative party voting. In studying any single election the dichotomy is easily made by trying out all the different possible combinations on each side until that particular combination is found which maximizes the ability of the resulting dichotomy to predict party choice in the election concerned.[1] Unfortunately, the dichotomy which best distinguishes Conservative from Labour supporters in one election may not be the same as that which best makes

---

[1] See Franklin and Mughan (1978) for a more detailed exposition of this procedure.

this distinction in another election.[2] So when studying party support over a number of elections we are faced with a problem that does not exist when studying single elections.

A straightforward solution to this problem, adopted for example by Rose (1974a) and by Franklin and Mughan (1978) is to ignore it, and construct different dichotomies for each election in so far as this is necessary to maximize the variance explained in party choice. However, a major purpose of this book is to try to relate changes in class voting to changes in social structure that occurred during the period under investigation; and in order to measure changes in the number of individuals having particular combinations of characteristics we need to retain the same definition of what constitutes each characteristic whenever we observe it. The nature of our standard measures has already been introduced in Chapter 3. What was not mentioned there was the cost of such standardization in terms of accurately representing the findings of each election study.

It would be encouraging to be able to report that much the same picture emerged whatever definitions were adopted or retained. Unfortunately, this is not the case. The relative importance of different variables at different elections does depend to some extent on the particular definitions which we adopt. In selecting the groupings of characteristics employed in each dichotomy we used two criteria. The first was to maximize the explanatory power of the dichotomy concerned in at least one of the elections studied, and the second (where we still had a choice after the first criterion had been fulfilled) was to choose dichotomies which, when taken together, led to a pattern of change in social structure that appeared intuitively reasonable. Happily, when the independent variables are summed into an additive index such as the one we employ in Chapter 4, differences in coding largely cancel out, and our overall findings on the changing nature of social influences on voting choice do not much depend on the

---

[2] This is because changes in electoral fortunes (which may have nothing to do with the influence of the particular variable concerned), by increasing or reducing the number of supporters for one of the major parties, may have the effect of increasing the correlation obtained when a larger or smaller number of characteristics are combined in that category of the dichotomy which is associated with support for the party concerned. There may also be substantive reasons associated with demographic change that would lead us to expect a smaller or larger grouping of characteristics to improve our ability to distinguish the supporters of one party from those of another.

particular coding scheme adopted for individual variables that make up the index.

The amount of explanatory power that we lose through the adoption of a standard coding scheme is graphically displayed in Figure 4.3. There, the broken line at the top of the chart showed how much variance we could have explained at each election by using the 'best' available coding of each variable, without regard to comparability. The difference between these figures and the best that can be obtained with a standard coding scheme (top-most solid line in the illustration) averages 0.038, or almost four per cent of variance explained, over the six elections depicted.

# REFERENCES

Alderman, Geoffrey (1978), *British Elections: Myth and Reality*, London: Batsford.

Asher, Herbert (1976), *Causal Modelling*, Beverly Hills: Sage.

Butler, David E. and Dennis Kavanagh (1974), *The British General Election of February 1974*, London: Macmillan.

– – and Anthony King (1965), *The British General Election of 1964*, London: Macmillan.

– – and Michael Pinto-Duschinsky (1971), *The British General Election of 1970*, London: Macmillan.

– – and Donald Stokes (1969, 1974), *Political Change in Britain: The Evolution of Electoral Choice*, 2nd edn. 1974, London: Macmillan.

Beer, Samuel H. (1965), *Modern British Politics*, London: Faber.

– – (1983), *Britain Against Itself*, London: Faber.

Calvert, Peter (1982), *The Concept of Class: An Historical Introduction*, London: Hutchinson.

Campbell, Angus *et al.* (1960), *The American Voter*, New York: Wiley.

Castells, M. (1978), *City, Class and Power*, London: Macmillan.

Cogan, Maurice (1978), *The Politics of Educational Change*, Glasgow: Fontana.

Craig, F. W. S. (1968), *British Parliamentary Election Statistics*, Glasgow: Political Reference Publications.

Crewe, Ivor, Bo Sarlvik, and James Alt (1977), 'Partisan Dealignment in Britain 1964–1974', *British Journal of Political Science* 7: 129–90.

Curtice, John and Michael Steed (1982), 'Electoral Choice and the Production of Government: The Changing Operation of the Electoral System in the United Kingdom since 1955', *British Journal of Political Science* 12: 249–98.

Dowse, R. E. and J. A. Hughes (1971), 'The Family, the School and the Socialization Process', *Sociology* 5: 21–46.

Draper, N. R. and H. Smith (1966), *Applied Regression Analysis*, New York: Wiley.

Drucker, Henry M. *et al.*, eds. (1983), *Developments in British Politics*, London: Macmillan.

Dunleavy, Patrick (1979), 'The Urban Basis of Political Alignment', *British Journal of Political Science* 9: 409–44.

– – (1980a), *Urban Political Analysis*, London: Macmillan.

– – (1980b), 'The Political Implications of Sectoral Cleavages and the Growth of State Employment' (two parts), *Political Studies* 28: 364–83 and 527–48.

– – (1980c), 'The Urban Basis of Political Alignment: A Rejoinder to Harrop', *British Journal of Political Science* 10: 398–402.

−− (1983), 'How to Decide How Voters Decide', *Politics* 2: 3–7.

Duverger, Maurice (1954), *Political Parties*, London: Methuen.

Edgell, S. and V. Duke (1983), 'Public Expenditure Cuts in Britain and Consumption Sectoral Cleavages', paper presented at the Political Studies Association conference, Newcastle.

Eijk, Cees Van der, and Cees Niemoller (1983), *Political Change in the Netherlands*, Amsterdam: Erasmus University Press.

Feist, Ursula, Manfred Gullrer, and Klaus Liepelt (1978), 'Structural Assimilation Versus Ideological Polarisation: On Changing Profiles of Political Parties in West Germany', in Max Kaase and Klaus von Beyme (eds.) *Sociopolitical Change and Participation in the West German Federal Election of 1976*, Beverly Hills: Sage, pp. 171–89.

Franklin, Mark N. (1982), 'Demographic and Political Components in the Decline of British Class Voting', *Electoral Studies* 1: 195–220.

−− (1983), 'The Rise of Issue Voting in British Elections', Glasgow: Strathclyde Papers on Government and Politics No. 3.

−− (1984), 'How the Decline of Class Voting Opened the Way to Radical Change in British Politics', *British Journal of Political Science* 14: 437–62.

− (1985), 'Assessing the Rise of Issue Voting in British Elections Since 1964', *Electoral Studies* 4: 36–55.

−− and Ronald Inglehart (1973), 'The British Electorate and Enoch Powell: A Strategy for Finding Dimensions in the Evaluation of a Political Personality', Reading: Political Studies Association.

−− and Anthony Mughan (1978), 'The Decline of Class Voting in Britain: Problems of Analysis and Interpretation', *American Political Science Review* 72: 523–34.

−− and Anthony Mughan (1980), 'In Defence of (Careful) Barefoot Empiricism', communication in the *American Political Science Review*, 74: 462–5.

−− and Edward Page (1984), 'A Critique of the Consumption Cleavage Approach in British Voting Studies', *Political Studies* 32: 521–36.

Goldberg, Arthur S. (1966), 'Discerning a Causal Pattern Among Data on Voting Behavior', *American Political Science Review* 60: 913–22.

Gordon, Robert A. (1968), 'Issues in Multiple Regression', *American Journal of Sociology* 73: 601–18.

Hanushek, Eric A. and John E. Jackson (1977), *Statistical Methods for Social Scientists*, London: Academic Press.

Harrop, Martin (1980), 'The Urban Basis of Political Alignment: A Comment', *British Journal of Political Science* 10: 388–98.

Howe, C. J. (1981), *Acquiring Language in a Conversational Context*, London: Academic Press.

Heath, Anthony (1981), *Social Mobility*, Glasgow: Fontana.

Hibbs, Douglas A., Jr. (1982), 'Economic Outcomes and Political Support for British Governments among Occupational Classes: A Dynamic Analysis', *American Political Science Review* 76: 259–79.

Himmelweit, Hilde T., Patrick Humphreys, Marianne Jaeger, and Michael Katz (1981), *How Voters Decide*, London: Academic Press.

Huckfeldt, R. Robert (1983), 'The Social Context of Political Change: Durability, Volatility, and Social Influence', *American Political Science Review* 77: 929–44.

Inglehart, Ronald (1971), 'The Silent Revolution in Europe: Inter-generational Change in Post-Industrial Societies', *American Political Science Review* 65: 991–1017.

— (1977), *The Silent Revolution: Changing Values and Political Styles among Western Publics*, New Jersey: Princeton University Press.

Jennings, M. Kent and Richard D. Niemi (1981), *Generations and Politics*, Princeton: University Press.

Kavanagh, Dennis (1983), *Political Science and Political Behaviour*, London: Allen and Unwin.

Katz, Richard S., Richard G. Niemi, and David Newman (1980), 'Reconstructing Past Partisanship in Britain', *British Journal of Political Science* 10: 505–15.

Kaufman, Herbert (1960), *The Forest Ranger*, Baltimore: Johns Hopkins University Press.

Key, V. O. Jr (1966), *The Responsible Electorate*, New York: Prentis Hall.

Kelley, Jonathan and Ian McAllister (1985), 'Social Context and Electoral Behaviour in Britain', *American Journal of Political Science* 29.

King, Anthony (1982), 'Whatever is Happening to the British Party System?', *Parliamentary Affairs* 35: 241–51.

Kirchheimer, Otto (1966), 'The Transformation of the Western European Party Systems' in J. LaPalombara and M. Weiner (eds.) *Political Parties and Political Development*, Princeton NJ: Princeton University Press.

Kramer, Gerald H. (1983), 'The Ecological Fallacy Revisited: Aggregate-Versus Individual-level Findings on Economics and Elections, and Sociotropic Voting', *American Political Science Review* 77: 92–111.

Le Grand, J. (1982), *The Strategy of Equality*, London: Allen and Unwin.

Lemieux, Peter H. (1977), 'Liberal Support in the February 1974 General Election', *Political Studies* 25: 323–42.

Lijphart, Arend (1975), *The Politics of Accommodation*, 2nd edn., Berkeley: University of California Press.

McAllister, Ian (1984), 'Housing Tenure and Party Choice in Australia, Britain and the United States', *British Journal of Political Science* 14: 509–22.

Margolis, Michael (1977), 'From Confusion to Confusion', *American Political Science Review* 71: 31–45.

Marsh, David (1971) 'Political Socialization: the Implicit Assumptions Questioned', *British Journal of Political Science* 1: 453–66.

Marwick, Arthur (1982), *British Society Since 1945*, London: A. Lane.

Meier, Kenneth J. and James E. Campbell (1979), 'Issue Voting: An Empirical Examination of Individually Necessary and Jointly Sufficient Conditions', *American Politics Quarterly* 7: 21–50.

Miller, William L. (1977), *Electoral Dynamics in Britain Since 1918*, London: Macmillan.

— — (1978), 'Social Class and Party Choice in England: A New Analysis', *British Journal of Political Science* 8: 257–84.

— — (1979), 'Class, Region and Strata at the British General Election of 1979', *Parliamentary Affairs* 32: 376–82.

Nie, Norman H., Sidney Verba, and John R. Petrocik (1976, 1981), *The Changing American Voter*, Cambridge Mass: Harvard University Press, 2nd edn. 1981.

— —, C. Hadlai Hull, Mark N. Franklin, *et al.* (1980), *SCSS: A User's Guide to the SCSS Conversational System*, New York: McGraw Hill.

Norton, Philip (1981), *The Commons in Perspective*, Oxford: Martin Robertson.

Page, Benjemin I. and Calvin C. Jones (1979), 'Reciprocal Effects of Policy Preferences, Party Loyalties and the Vote', *American Political Science Review* 73: 1071–89.

Pateman, Carole (1980), 'The Civic Culture: A Philosophic Critique' in G. A. Almond and S. Verba *The Civic Culture Revisited*, Boston: Little Brown.

Pulzer, Peter (1967), *Political Representation and Elections in Britain*, London: Allen and Unwin.

Rasmussen, Jorgen (1981), 'David Steel's Liberals: Too Old to Cry, Too Hurt to Laugh' in Howard R. Penniman (ed.) *Britain at the Polls*, Washington: American Enterprise Institute.

Robinson, W. S. (1950), 'Ecological Correlations and the Behaviour of Individuals' *American Sociological Review* 15: 351–7.

Rokkan, Stein (1972), *Citizens, Elections, Parties*, Oslo: Universitetsforlaget Oslo.

Rose, Richard (1968), 'Class and Party Divisions: Britain as a Test Case', *Sociology* 1: 129–62.

— — (1974a), *The Problem of Party Government*, London: Macmillan.

— — (1974b), 'Britain: Simple Abstractions and Complex Realities' in Richard Rose (ed.) *Electoral Behavior: A Comparative Handbook*, New York: Free Press.

— — (1980), *Politics in England: An Interpretation for the 1980's*, London: Faber and Faber.

Sarlvik, Bo and Ivor Crewe (1983), *Decade of Dealignment*, London: Macmillan.

Sartori, Giovanni (1969), 'From the Sociology of Politics to Political Sociology' in S. M. Lipset (ed.) *Politics and the Social Sciences*, London: Oxford University Press.

Saunders, Peter (1981), *Social Theory and the Urban Question*, London: Hutchinson.

— — (1982), 'Beyond Housing Classes: The Sociological Significance of

Property Rights in Means of Consumption', University of Sussex Urban and Regional Studies Working Paper 33.

Schattschneider, E. E. (1960), *The Semi-Sovereign People*, New York: Holt Rineheart and Winston.

Sonquist, John A., Elizabeth Lau Baker, and James N. Morgan (1971), *Searching for Structure*, Ann Arbor: Institute for Social Research.

Steed, Michael (1974), 'The Results Analysed' in Butler and Kavanagh (1974) Appendix 2.

Stokes, Donald E. (1969), 'Cross-Level Inference as a Game Against Nature' in J. L. Bernd (ed.) *Mathematical Applications in Political Science II*, Charlottesville: University of Virginia Press.

— (1974), 'Compound Paths: An Expository Note', *American Journal of Political Science* 18: 191-214.

Sumner, William Graham (1916), *Folkways: A Study of the Sociological Importance of Usages, Manners, Customs, Mores and Morals*, New Haven: Yale University Press 1916.

Toffler, Alvin (1981), *The Third Wave*, London: Pan.

Tuckel, Peter S. and Felipe Tejera (1983), 'Changing Patterns in American Voting Behavior, 1914-1980', *Public Opinion Quarterly* 47: 143-302.

Whiteley, Paul (1983), *The Labour Party in Crisis*, London: Methuen.

# INDEX